MAKE MINE MUSIC!

written and illustrated by

Tom Walther

Little, Brown and Company
Boston   *Toronto*

Thanks to the friends, family, and music people who aided directly
and indirectly in the creation of this book, especially Jenefer Merrill and the
Exploratorium gang, Don Hewitt, the kids at Edison and John Swett Schools in
San Francisco, the Alvarado Arts Program, the Community Music Center
of San Francisco, Geri and our San Francisco Symphony friends, Sarah Campsey,
and George and Penny Kahumoku. Special thanks to David Reck for his book
Music of the Whole Earth and the Diagram Group for creating the book
Musical Instruments of the World, both of which stimulated quantum leaps
in my musical instrument vision. Several of the excellent illustrations in
Musical Instruments of the World were adapted for this book.

This Brown Paper School book was edited and prepared
for publication at the Yolla Bolly Press, Covelo, California,
during the spring of 1980. The series is under the supervision
of James and Carolyn Robertson. Production staff:
Dan Hibshman, Joyca Cunnan, Barbara Speegle, Leslie
Combest, Diana Fairbanks, and James Bequette.

First edition. Published simultaneously in Canada
by Little, Brown & Company (Canada) Limited.
Printed in the United States of America.

Library of Congress Cataloging in Publication Data

Walther, Tom.
Make mine music.

SUMMARY: Discusses a variety of musical instruments
and presents directions for making and playing them.
1. Musical instruments—Construction—Juvenile
literature. [1. Musical instruments] I. Title.
ML460.W24   781.91   80-23600
ISBN 0-316-92111-4
ISBN 0-316-92112-2 (pbk.)

For Geri
and all of you who let your music
light the world

Contents

Introduction
Music Is Something You Can Make
page 9

Chapter 1
Making Sound Discoveries
page 10

Chapter 2
A Music Alphabet
page 16

Chapter 3
Tools for Making Music
page 18

Chapter 4
You Can Get Started on a Shoestring
page 22

Chapter 5
What's an Idiophone?
page 56

Chapter 6
Slappin' Skins
page 83

Chapter 7
Blowin' in the Winds
page 89

Chapter 8
Body Music
page 114

Chapter 9
Musical Notations
page 120

Chapter 10
Science, Music, and You
page 123

Some Books About Musical Instruments
page 125

Things You Can Make

How to Make a Musical Bow, page 24

Two Ways to Add a Resonator to Your Bow, page 25

How to Make a Gutbucket, page 28

How to Make a Monochord, page 29

How to Make a Sound Box, page 32

How to Make a Lyre, page 35

How to Make a Harp, page 38

How to Make a Lute, page 42

How to Make a Spike Fiddle, page 46

How to Make an Aeolian Harp, page 54

How to Make an Ear Zither, page 55

Flowerpot Bells and Nail Chimes, page 60

How to Make Marimbas, page 71

How to Make Magical Marimba Resonators, page 74

A Tubular Glockenspiel, page 76

How to Make a Thumb Piano, page 80

How to Make a Slit Drum, page 82

How to Make Carpet-Tube Bongos, page 86

How to Make a Lion's Roar, page 87

How to Make a Bull-Roarer, page 90

Buzz Disc-O, page 91

How to Make Panpipes in the Key of C, page 94

How to Make a Simple Flute, page 95

Disturbing Parts of Whistles, page 98

A Sliding Trumpet, page 110

Make an Inhuman Vocal Tract, page 116

How to Make a Composition Board, page 122

Introduction

Music Is Something
You Can Make

Music is something you can make. You can make sounds, sing songs, and use special tools called instruments to play more sounds and songs. This book is loaded with ideas about making music, especially about making musical instruments work. If you ever wondered how musical instruments work, this book is for you.

You will also learn how to make many instruments that you can actually play. The world around you is brimming with materials with musical possibilities that you can make into your own instruments.

You will learn what music is made of and some ways to share your musical ideas with others. You will gain some sound knowledge that will open the door of the world of music to you.

Perhaps you think music is just for special people and that only special people can understand it. It is. Music is for special people just like you.

Chapter 1
Making Sound Discoveries

In 1492 Christopher Columbus and his crew wandered across the sea and found North and South America. We say he discovered them. But he didn't invent them or make them up. He had the imagination and courage to travel to places that nobody from his part of the world had ever seen before. Because of his discovery, people began to see the world in a different way.

Sounds are the building blocks of music. There are billions of sounds happening all around the earth every instant. Some of them will be as new to you as the New World was to Columbus. But you don't need to sail away.

Wherever you are, you can explore this world of sounds, including some you may never have noticed before.

With a notebook or piece of paper on your lap and a pencil in your hand, sit quietly with your eyes closed. As you hear different sounds, list them on your paper. Make lists as you sit in different places. Sounds in the garden may be very different from sounds in the kitchen just a short distance away. Listen in quiet places. Listen in noisy places. Try this activity with some friends. Do they notice sounds that you did not? The world seems a different place when you discover new sounds in it.

MAKE A SOUND QUIZ AND TRY IT OUT WITH YOUR FRIENDS.

MATCH THE SOUND WITH THE SOURCE:	
DOG	MEOW
HORSE EATING	TAT-TAT-TAT
SPORTS CAR	SCREECH
THUNDER	CRASH
CAT	RUMBLE
RAIN	URROOOM
BRAKES	BANG
BIRD	CLOMP
DISH BREAKING	RUFF
FIRECRACKER	AH-CHOO
NOSE	SWISH
BOOTS ON WOOD	CHOMP
BROOM	CHIRP

A Sound Is Worth a Thousand Words

You have probably heard the saying "a picture is worth a thousand words." It's not necessary to use lots of words when a picture can explain something just as well. The same is true of sounds. Sounds can tell you more than just squeak, whoosh, or buzz. A particular squeak tells you that the bathroom door is being opened. The whoosh says the car that just zoomed past was going fast. A certain buzzing tells you, as you are about to drop off to sleep, that a mosquito is exploring your room and is interested in your blood.

Sounds are not just there; they help you know what is going on in the world. When a dog growls a deep, gurgling snarl behind the door you just knocked on, you immediately feel a chill creep up your spine. When you hear the chuckling of laughter, you instantly feel warm and tickled inside. Nobody has to say anything. From just the sound you get the message.

The fact that sounds can have meanings is an important reason people make and listen to music. As you notice sounds, wonder what they are telling you about the world around you. Notice how they make you feel. You are on your way to discovering music.

Fffft! Sssssh! Beep!

Take a look at that list of sounds you made and notice how you described what you heard. You may have told how the sound was made: John made a noise with his mouth. Someone opened the door. You may have noticed what made the sound: Mother walking upstairs, a bird, or a car going by.

When you sat and listened to different sounds, did you use any words like cough, creak, clomp, chirp, tweet, or whoosh? Some words sound like the sound they describe. These words have a special name. They are called onomatopoeia (say ono-mata-peea). They are especially useful when you need to tell someone about sounds. They are also useful for explaining things you see, imagine, and feel.

Think of more words that sound like sounds—sounds you hear at school, along the street, in a park, sounds from a factory, farm, or kitchen. Imagine the sounds you hear at a baseball game or car race, when you are sewing, washing dishes, or sleeping.

What Makes a Sound?

A sound begins with the movement of one thing hitting another. A spoon tapping a plate is one way; your foot stomping the floor is another. The movement can be as tiny as a mosquito flapping its wings or as gigantic as an earthquake shaking a mountain.

Everything in our world is composed of tiny molecules. Things like steel and rocks are made of molecules that are tightly packed. Substances like air and water have loosely packed molecules. These differences in how molecules are packed make some matter bouncy and elastic and some hard and rigid.

SET UP A ROW OF DOMINOES OR BLOCKS. THEN GIVE THE END ONE A PUSH AND WATCH THE PULSE TRAVEL DOWN THE ROW.

When any object is hit, its molecules are jarred and made to move about. Because the object hit is then moving, it bumps into the air molecules around it and causes them to shake. As these disturbed air molecules bump into others near them, a small tremor, or shaking motion, is passed through the

air in all directions. When the tremor reaches your eardrums and causes *them* to vibrate, your "hearing" of sound begins.

The repeated back-and-forth shaking of something is called vibration. When vibrations shake at a rate of between 20 and 20,000 in a second—with enough strength to move the molecules of air next to your eardrums just one ten-thousand-millionth of an inch—your ears can hear them.

When something vibrates at a rate slower than 20 or faster than 20,000 per second, you cannot hear it, but a sound is still being made. Cats can hear vibrations between 60 and 65,000 per second, and dogs hear in a range between 15 and 50,000. This is the reason some animals can hear special whistles that people can't.

The universe is filled with repeating-motion events happening at speeds slower or faster than sound. Light and color are very fast vibrations you can detect with your eyes. You taste and smell vibrations of the molecules of things you eat. Vibrations of sound are much slower than these vibrations. Repeating motions like walking, chewing, and shaking hands happen at speeds much slower than sound.

KEEP GOING ↑

IF YOU MADE A STACK 464 MILES TALL OF SHEETS OF PAPER AS THICK AS THIS PAGE, THEN SQUEEZED THE STACK DOWN SO IT HAD AS MANY SHEETS BUT WAS ONLY AN INCH TALL, EACH SHEET IN THE STACK WOULD

BE 1/10,000,000,000 (ONE TEN-THOUSAND-MILLIONTH) OF AN INCH THICK.

WHEN THE MOLECULES OF AIR NEXT TO YOUR EARDRUM VIBRATE 1/10,000,000,000 OF AN INCH, YOU CAN HEAR THEM.

↑ TOP 464 MI

A Sound
Gets Around

You can get an idea of how sound travels by filling a pan (a baking pan or frying pan will do) with water. Set the pan on a table and do something else until the water becomes perfectly still. Then touch the water with your fingertip, a pencil, or even a pin. Notice what happens in the water as you make your *tiny* disturbance. The disturbance moves through the water and forms waves. The waves you see on the surface of the water are the most visible result of your touch, but you have also disturbed every molecule of water in the pan, the molecules of the pan, and the molecules of air around the pan.

As you touch the water, try to count the number of waves you see form in a second. The moving water doesn't cause sound because the motion of the waves is too slow. Do you think the molecules of water that you touched are the same ones that bounced against the sides of the pan?

With a rope you can get a good view of how a tremor or disturbance travels. You hold one end of the rope, while a friend holds the other end. Stretch the rope (not too tightly) between you. One of you shakes your end of the rope with

MARKER

a quick flick of the wrist. Can you see a wave pass through the rope? Try a series of fast flicks. Now a series of slow ones. Shake the end of the rope hard, then softly, and watch the changing vibrations.

Put a mark with chalk or a piece of tape on the rope and imagine that it is a molecule. Notice how it moves as the waves pass along the rope. The motion you are observing is called wave motion. It is the way sound travels. When a musical instrument is played it sends a tremor through the air. That tremor causes waves in the air similar to but much faster than the waves you saw in the pan. Each molecule only moves back and forth a short distance.

Many other things travel in wave motion besides sound. Light, electricity, radio and TV signals, fish, birds, and even people make waves in their journeys. The back-and-forth motion you make as you flap your hand to signal goodby to a friend is a wave motion. In fact, if you could move your hand back and forth (or up and down) 20 or more times per second you would send a tremor traveling through the air that you could hear. A mosquito flaps its wings fast enough for you to hear them.

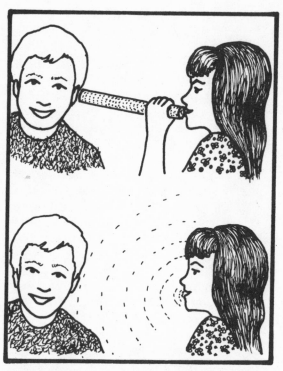

Can You Hear Me?

Sound travels in all directions from its source. Because of this, only a small amount of the sounds energy reaches your ear. You can see the difference this makes by talking through a tube.

Get a tube like the kind wrapping paper comes on. First have a friend talk to you through the open air. Then have her talk to you just as loud through the tube. Which sounds louder?

When your friend spoke into the tube, the energy from her voice was not permitted to go in all directions—you heard concentrated sound. If other people were standing nearby, they may have heard nothing. Without the tube they would have gotten a share of the sound energy.

"I'm Just Passing Through."

In order for a sound to travel from its source to your ear it must travel through something. The something that sound travels through is called a medium. The most common medium for the sounds you hear on earth is the sea of air that surrounds the planet. Air has a special elastic (bouncy) quality that makes it a good medium. Materials such as water, wood, steel, the earth, and bone are good media too. Materials such as cloth, foam rubber, cork, and cotton are soft and have many separate little pockets of air that interrupt and break up sound waves. Because they absorb sound, they do not make good media.

At sea level when the air is 32° F., sound travels 1,090 feet per second through it. When it is hotter, molecules of air move faster and sound travels faster through them. Sound travels four times faster through water than through air. Through steel it travels sixteen times faster than through air.

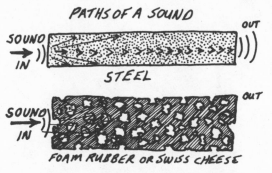

PATHS OF A SOUND

SOUND IN →)) STEEL OUT)))

SOUND IN → FOAM RUBBER OR SWISS CHEESE OUT

You can make some listening devices using media through which sound travels quickly. Steel, sticks, rocks, and other hard materials have molecules that are closely and evenly packed. The closer and more evenly spaced the molecules are, the faster sound can travel through them. By holding one end of a steel rod or a thin wooden stick against your ear and the other against the chest of a friend, you can hear his heartbeat. Mechanics use a similar device to locate the exact spot where something is clunking in a roaring car engine. By holding a listening stick against a wall, you can sometimes hear the conversation going on in the next room. Native Americans used to listen for approaching hoof beats by putting one ear to the ground. They could hear a rider coming long before he could be seen or heard by listening in the air.

The materials musical instruments are made of are selected because of their ability to make, carry, and project sounds.

Chapter 2

A Music Alphabet

There are some special words used to describe music that are used in this book that some people find confusing. Music is a kind of language, and like any language it has an alphabet. In fact, in different lands musicians have entirely different musical alphabets.

The thing common to all music is sound. In particular parts of the world certain sounds are selected to be the alphabet from which the musical stories of that land are composed.

In North and South America and Europe our basic musical alphabet is made up of twelve tones. These twelve tones have letter names: A, B flat, B, C, C sharp, D, D sharp, E, F, F sharp, G, G sharp, then the next scale begins with A prime. Each of these separate tones is called a note. The notes together form a scale. On the piano the notes with just a letter name are played on the white keys. The notes that have sharp or flat in their names are played on the black keys.

In 1928 the British and French got together and decided to agree on some musical matters. They agreed that the note that makes 440 vibrations per second would be called A. So the other notes of the scale vibrate in proportion to the 440 A. The proportion of vibra-

tions between each of the consecutive notes of the scale is called a half-step. This scale is not the only one in the world, but it is the one most of the songs you commonly hear are made of.

The note A prime vibrates twice as fast as A, and we say it is an octave higher. The next A up the scale, A double prime, vibrates three times as fast as A and is two octaves higher. A piano has 88 notes for a range of 7⅓ octaves.

When two, three, or more different notes are played at the same time, they make a chord, much as the letters of the alphabet can be grouped together to make a word. Chords often have particular feelings and meanings, just like words. Notes and chords are arranged into compositions or musical stories, just as letters and words are arranged into verbal stories.

Some other words you will hear to describe music are: bass, baritone, tenor, alto, and soprano. These refer to low, high, and in-the-middle ranges of sound. Instruments or people that produce deep, low, slowly vibrating notes are basses. Baritones produce a range that is low but not so low as basses. Men with deep voices are usually basses or baritones. The tuba plays music in the bass range. The cello plays mostly in the baritone range. Men with medium-high voices are usually tenors. The trombone often plays in the tenor range. Women with medium voices usually sing and speak in the alto range. Violas and English horns play in this range. Women with high-pitched voices are sopranos, and violins and flutes are soprano-voiced instruments.

Timbre, a Sound Quality

A sound can be loud or soft. It has a pitch or frequency. Sounds also have individual qualities. The individual qualities of a sound are called its timbre (pronounced tam-burr). Timbre is something you hear all the time.

If both a piano and a trumpet play a note that vibrates the air molecules next to your eardrum 440 times a second, we would say they are both playing A. This would be true, but it doesn't tell the whole story. You could tell which sound came from the trumpet and which came from the piano. A trumpet just doesn't sound like a piano, even when they are in tune and playing the same note. If you stop and think about it, a trumpet and a piano can't actually play the same note. The piano plays its A and the trumpet plays its A. What they can do is play at the same pitch. Timbre is a sum, not a part of a sound. It is much like the answer to an addition problem.

    pitch
+ loudness
+ harmonics
+ how the materials the instrument is made of vibrate
+ source of the sound
+ place where the sound is played
= *timbre*

As you test things in your environment for their musical qualities, notice changes in timbre.

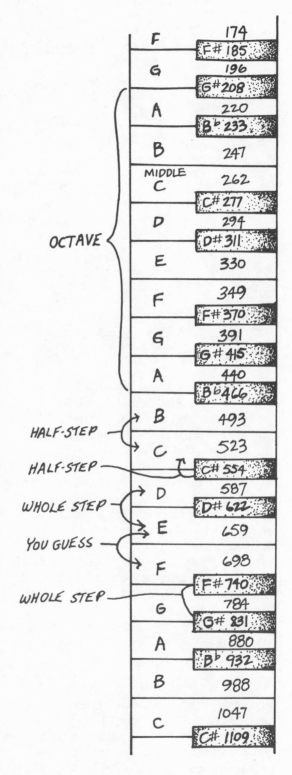

17

Chapter 3

Tools for Making Music

SUPPORT YOUR WORK
TO SAW, CHISEL, DRILL, OR HAMMER

TREE FORK VISE BENCH HOOK STOOL STEPS

Some of the projects in this book involve using tools. Some will even involve your making tools. That's because musical instruments are, in fact, tools for making sound.

In the activities of this book you will use saws, hammers, nails, files and rasps, drills, screwdrivers, and other tools. Many of them are probably already around the place where you live. Getting good at using tools will teach you skills you'll use all your life. Remember that a tool isn't a weapon, but it can hurt you or somebody else if it's not used correctly.

Following are some lessons on how to use tools safely and effectively.

Saw Tips

A saw will be handy for some of the projects in this book. There are many kinds of saws. They come in a variety of shapes and sizes to do different jobs. They will all work well if you observe these five principles.

1. *Relax*. Saws are designed to help, not to hurt you. Think of a saw, or any tool, as a friend. Tools work better if you treat them with care and respect.

2. *Pay attention* to what you are doing. Know where your fingers, toes, and the saw are. Saws, even friendly ones, sometimes cut people who aren't paying attention.

3. *Look at the teeth*. (This is also a good thing to do when you are buying a horse.) Saw teeth have a slanted side and a vertical side. All saws cut as you push or pull the vertical side of the teeth into the wood. The teeth slide across the wood as you pull or push them against the slanted side.

4. *Support your work*.

5. *Push gently and firmly*. If you push too hard, the saw's teeth will jam and the saw won't move. When you get stuck, relax; then pull the saw in the slanted direction and begin to saw lightly. You can add pressure as you get going.

HOW TO USE A COPING SAW

The Amazing Coping Saw

Did you ever wonder how to cut out a shape in the middle of a board without sawing in from the edge? The coping saw is the answer. Remove the blade from the saw frame. Then use a drill and drill a little hole in the board. Put the blade through the hole and attach the saw frame to it again. Now cut out the shape you want. When you have finished cutting, remove the blade from the frame and take it out of the hole. In several projects in this book, the coping saw will make problems disappear.

If you have to buy a saw to do the projects in this book, definitely the kind to get is a coping saw. The coping saw is suited for light work. It is an easy size to handle, and it can do amazing things like cut circles or irregular shapes. It is a fairly inexpensive tool.

Coping saws have a thin blade that is stretched across a U-shaped frame. To change blades you relax the tension by unscrewing the handle. Be careful when you loosen the handle not to twist the blade. Hold the little metal bar near the handle to keep the saw blade straight.

To turn the blade loosen the handle and turn both metal bars near the ends of the blade at the same time. If you turn just one, you will twist and perhaps break the blade.

The saw works best if you hold your board so you are working near the edge of a bench or table that supports it. Don't push the blade against the wood too hard. If you do, the blade will jam and bend; so if the blade jams, back off, relax, and start sawing again—lightly.

Holy Drill Thrills

Drills are used to make smooth, neat holes in things; they come in several varieties: the brace and bit, electric drill, eggbeater type, and the Yankee drill. Of these, the best drills for the projects in this book are the eggbeater type and the Yankee drill. For large holes the brace and bit is best. If you are going to use an electric drill, get some adult help.

Drills are quite safe if you use good sense. Always have some scrap wood under what you are drilling so you won't ruin a table, floor, or the drill bits. The blade part of the drill is called the bit. Bits of different widths can be fitted into the same drill. The hole a drill makes will be as wide as the bit: a ½-inch bit makes a ½-inch hole.

Pay attention to what you are doing. Keep the bit going straight. It helps to start the hole by punching a small dent (with a nail) right where you want the center of the hole to be. Aim the tip of

WAYS TO MAKE A HOLE

YANKEE DRILL

EGGBEATER HAND DRILL

BRACE AND BIT

COLD CHISEL

NAIL

AWL

KNIFE

ELECTRIC DRILL

BE CAREFUL WITH ALL SHARP TOOLS

TIN SNIPS

COPING SAW

SCRAP TO PROTECT TABLE AND DRILL

the bit into the dent. This keeps the drill bit from wandering all over when you begin drilling the hole.

You can make holes in tin cans by hammering a nail through the tin. If you need to make a larger hole in a can, use a cold chisel (a chisel made for metal) and a hammer to cut an X or a V, then bend the metal flaps over with a screwdriver or pliers. Tin cans cut; wear gloves to protect your hands.

Raspicious Beasts

Files and rasps are very handy for shaping wood and metal. Metal files have fine teeth, and wood rasps have rougher ones. For roughing out shapes use a rough file. Then smooth it with a file with finer teeth. To cut with a file you push it. The teeth work on the same principle as a saw. You push to cut; when you pull, the teeth slide. Look at the teeth of the file you are using to see which direction to push.

If you are going to buy a file, get a "4 in 1." It has four different cutting sur-

FILES AND RASPS

FLAT   ENDVIEW →

HALF-ROUND

ROUND OR RATTAIL

4 IN 1 OR COMBINATION

faces on one tool and is handy for lots of jobs. For filing inside holes a 3/8-inch rattail, or round, file is handy.

All tools need to be handled with care, especially those with cutting edges, such as knives, chisels, and saws. Remember to work so the sharp edges point away from you. And be sure they aren't pointing at a friend. Know where you (all parts of you) are, where tables, floors, and your friends are when you are working around them. If you need help, ask an adult. Treat tools like friends: enjoy and respect them.

Chapter 4

You Can Get Started on a Shoestring

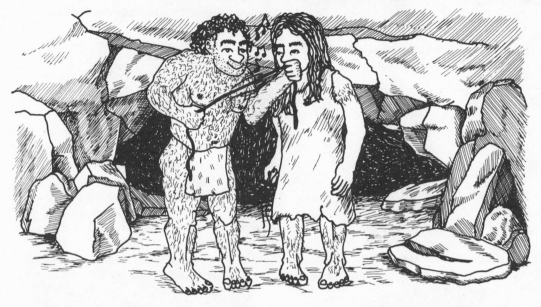

Thousands of years ago someone stretched a string and discovered it could make a sound. With this simple discovery a huge family of musical instruments was born. The imaginations of people in different times and places have been tickled and inspired by the simple magic of the singing string.

Singing strings can be made of all sorts of materials; plastics, plant fibers, animal hair, vines, wire, and animal intestines are a few. A quick check around your house and neighborhood will yield a variety of strings just waiting to sing.

You do not need a lot of money, fancy tools, or special skills to begin to build musical instruments. You can literally start this adventure on a shoestring. If your shoes do not have laces, any string will do—so will a piece of light wire, a leather thong, or a rubber band. Make it about 1 foot long.

The Fabulous String

Stretch your string between your hands. Then give it a flip with your thumb. Watch the string vibrate. Feel the vibrations from the string pass into your hands. Listen for the sound it makes. Move the string closer to your ear and notice that the sound is louder.

To transfer the vibrations of the string directly to your ear, hold one end of the string against the flap of your ear. As you stretch the string tight, give it another flip with your thumb. You will hear a sound. This is an instrument you can play with!

Notice the changes in the sound of the string as you relax or tighten your instrument. You are hearing the *pitch* of the string change. Pitch refers to the number of times a sound vibrates in a second. As you pull your string tight, its pitch becomes higher. This means it vibrates more times per second. As you relax the tension on the string, it vibrates more slowly. It makes a lower number of vibrations per second, so we say its pitch is lower.

Because you can change the pitch of your string, you can actually play a tune on it. "Mary Had a Little Lamb" is a good one to try. Hum it first. Then sing it through in your mind. Now as you sing the song in your mind, tighten or loosen the string so the string's sounds match the sounds you are imagining. To get the feel of this try it several times.

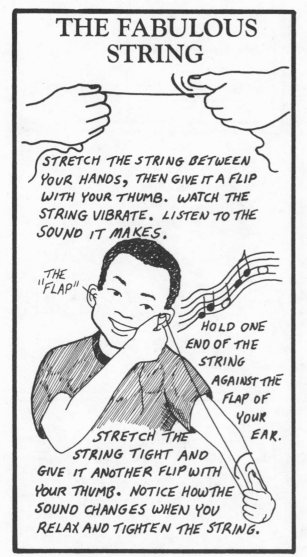

THE FABULOUS STRING

STRETCH THE STRING BETWEEN YOUR HANDS, THEN GIVE IT A FLIP WITH YOUR THUMB. WATCH THE STRING VIBRATE. LISTEN TO THE SOUND IT MAKES.

THE "FLAP"

HOLD ONE END OF THE STRING AGAINST THE FLAP OF YOUR EAR.

STRETCH THE STRING TIGHT AND GIVE IT ANOTHER FLIP WITH YOUR THUMB. NOTICE HOW THE SOUND CHANGES WHEN YOU RELAX AND TIGHTEN THE STRING.

Discover what music you can play with your particular string. How many different sounds can you make? One great advantage of this musical instrument—the fabulous string—is that nobody else can hear what you are playing. It will not bother anyone if you try things over and over. But the fabulous string has a great disadvantage too. Imagine you have practiced for a while and are proud as a peacock of your musical ability. If you are like just about everyone else on earth, you want to share your music with somebody. The now not-quite-so-fabulous string is a private musical instrument.

You have an instrumental problem. But a problem is often a place where adventure can begin. Your problem with the quiet string is no exception. You can solve it with a stick!

Stick Meets String

The simplest musical bows consist of a string fastened to the ends of a flexible stick. They are played by plucking the string with the finger or a pick, tapping it with a stick, or rubbing it with a second bow.

Some people speculate that the musical bow was adapted from the hunting bow. A hunter heard the twang of his bowstring and probably began to play with its sound. It is also possible that an ancient musician discovered she could shoot arrows with her musical bow.

Many musical bows are not bows at all. In some the string is stretched along a straight stick, then a bridge is placed between the stick and the string. The bridge is usually made of a small piece of wood, but seashells, stones, and gourds are also used. The bridge helps to stretch the string. It also allows the string to vibrate freely. In other bows the string is held away from a straight stick by a tuning peg.

HOW TO MAKE A MUSICAL BOW

ALL YOU NEED IS A STICK AND STRING.

THE STICK SHOULD BE LONGER THAN A FOOT, SHORTER THAN YOU, AND STRONG.

THE STICK (ABOUT ¾ INCH THICK)

ONE FOOT

TWO FEET

IT SHOULD BEND INTO A GENTLE ARCH WITHOUT BREAKING.

ARCH WHEN BENT

A THICKER STICK WITH A __NATURAL__ ARCH IS ALSO OK.

THE STRING MUST BE STRONG SO YOU CAN PULL IT TIGHT. YOU CAN USE:
• NYLON FISHING LINE
• WIRE
• COTTON CORD
• PLASTIC STRINGS
• GUITAR STRINGS
• BANJO STRINGS
• ANY STRONG STRING
CUT A LENGTH AT LEAST A FOOT LONGER THAN YOUR STICK.

① TIE ONE END OF THE STRING TO ONE END OF YOUR STICK.

② STRETCH THE STRING TO THE OTHER END OF THE STICK AS YOU BEND THE STICK INTO AN ARCH. WRAP THE STRING AROUND THE STICK 3 OR 4 TIMES SO IT WON'T SLIP, THEN TIE IT WITH A KNOT.

PRESTO, PLUCKO, YOU HAVE A MUSICAL BOW!

③ HOLD YOUR BOW AS SHOWN. THE STRING LIES ACROSS YOUR OPEN MOUTH, TOUCHING IT AT THE UPPER CORNER. PLUCK THE STRING WITH YOUR LOWER THUMB OR EITHER INDEX FINGER. ADJUST YOUR MOUTH TO MAKE THE SOUND LOUDER. BEND THE BOW TO CHANGE THE PITCH.

PLUCK WITH YOUR THUMB HERE.

SOME WAYS TO ATTACH THE STRING TO A BOW

HOLE   SLOT   NOTCH   GROOVE   WRAPPED   TUNING PEG   COMBINATION

YOU CAN DECORATE YOUR BOW WITH PAINT, WHITTLING, FEATHERS, OR YARN.

TWO WAYS TO ADD A RESONATOR TO YOUR BOW

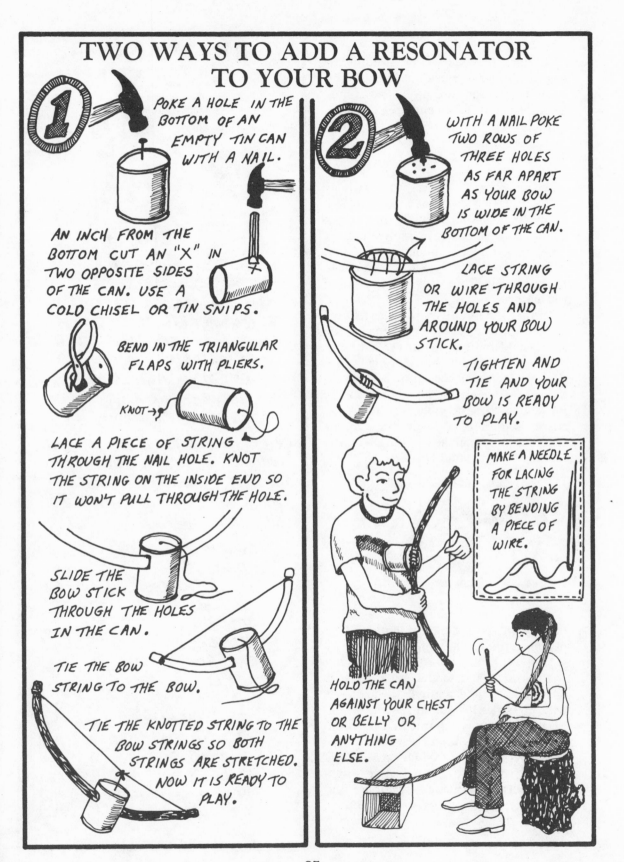

1 POKE A HOLE IN THE BOTTOM OF AN EMPTY TIN CAN WITH A NAIL.

AN INCH FROM THE BOTTOM CUT AN "X" IN TWO OPPOSITE SIDES OF THE CAN. USE A COLD CHISEL OR TIN SNIPS.

BEND IN THE TRIANGULAR FLAPS WITH PLIERS.

KNOT→

LACE A PIECE OF STRING THROUGH THE NAIL HOLE. KNOT THE STRING ON THE INSIDE END SO IT WON'T PULL THROUGH THE HOLE.

SLIDE THE BOW STICK THROUGH THE HOLES IN THE CAN.

TIE THE BOW STRING TO THE BOW.

TIE THE KNOTTED STRING TO THE BOW STRINGS SO BOTH STRINGS ARE STRETCHED. NOW IT IS READY TO PLAY.

2 WITH A NAIL POKE TWO ROWS OF THREE HOLES AS FAR APART AS YOUR BOW IS WIDE IN THE BOTTOM OF THE CAN.

LACE STRING OR WIRE THROUGH THE HOLES AND AROUND YOUR BOW STICK.

TIGHTEN AND TIE AND YOUR BOW IS READY TO PLAY.

MAKE A NEEDLE FOR LACING THE STRING BY BENDING A PIECE OF WIRE.

HOLD THE CAN AGAINST YOUR CHEST OR BELLY OR ANYTHING ELSE.

Since the string is wound around the peg the player can use the peg to tighten or loosen the tension of the string. Changing the tension changes the pitch of the string.

Louder, Louder

When you make your musical bow, you will notice it is not a loud instrument. Because the string is thin, it can shake only a few air molecules. In order to get more molecules shaking, devices of several types are added to the basic bow. These devices are called resonators.

The human mouth can be a resonator for the musical bow. The stick of the bow is held against the player's mouth. The player varies the size of his mouth opening to make sounds produced by the vibrating string and bow louder. Bows can also be held against your chest, abdomen, a large tin can, or anything that encloses a volume of air, to make them sound louder.

An ideal bow for the lazy musician is played on the island of Guam. The player actually lies on his back to play a long musical bow. Half a coconut shell is attached to the stick, and its open side is held against the player's belly to make the sound resonate.

You can take your musical bow and go resonance hunting. Resonances live in all sorts of unlikely places. Hold the stick of your bow against doors, windows, suitcases, couch cushions, and other objects and observe which ones produce the loudest and richest sounds.

RESONANCE'S RESIDENCES

WITH YOUR MUSICAL BOW YOU CAN HUNT FOR RESONANT QUALITIES. SEE WHAT THINGS AND PLACES HELP IT SOUND BEST AND LOUDEST. HOLD THE BOW AGAINST WINDOWS, FLOORS, DOORS. FIND OUT WHICH SURFACES CAUSE THE STRING TO MAKE MORE SOUND.

CHECK THE PLACES ON THIS LIST AND NUMBER THEM FROM LOUDEST TO SOFTEST. GUESS FIRST, THEN CHECK WITH YOUR BOW. YOU MAY BE SURPRISED.

___ COUCH CUSHION
___ WINDOW
___ HOLLOW DOOR
___ TABLE   ↖ GUESS COLUMN ↓
___ PILLOW
___ SUITCASE
___ CARDBOARD BOX
___ WALL
___ BED
___ KITCHEN FLOOR
___ RUG
___ CURTAINS
___ YOUR CHEST
___ AGAINST YOUR EAR
___ PIE TIN

SOME UNBOWED MUSICAL BOWS

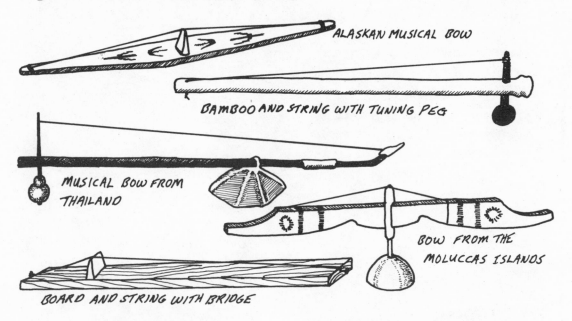

ALASKAN MUSICAL BOW

BAMBOO AND STRING WITH TUNING PEG

MUSICAL BOW FROM THAILAND

BOW FROM THE MOLUCCAS ISLANDS

BOARD AND STRING WITH BRIDGE

Single-String Harps

Your growing collection of stringed instruments includes the fabulous string and the musical bow. Now you are ready for the bigtime! Discover the single-string harps. The all-American classic of this group is the washtub bass, or "gutbucket." Probably this name refers to the instrument's catgut strings, which are actually made from sheep gut, and its bucket (washtub) resonator. Other than string and some kind of bucket, all you need to make your single-string harp is a stick, a hole, and a couple of knots.

Big galvanized washtubs, once part of everybody's laundry and bathing equipment, are becoming somewhat rare. New ones can be purchased at a hardware store, but they are expensive. If you can find a beat-up one nobody wants to use, you're lucky. But if you are out of luck, use some imagination and look around to come up with a substitute. A large coffee can, garbage can, garbage can lid, bucket, or a box are some possibilities.

For a string almost any kind will do. Choose a piece of string or wire you think suits the instrument you build.

An old broomstick is often used for the handle of the washtub bass, but you can choose any stick that works for you and still be true to the oldtime spirit of the gutbucket.

Playing Your Gutbucket

Get ready to play your gutbucket by placing the notch in the bottom end of the stick over the rim around the bottom of the bucket. Place one foot on the rim of the bucket to hold the resonator down as you stretch the string. If you have made one of the smaller models (with a coffee can, for instance) it will probably work better to hold the can under your arm or between your legs. The idea is to get the string stretched and still have enough hands left over to vary the pitch by pushing and pulling the stick or by sliding your stick-holding hand up and down the stick with the string gripped in it.

Sound the instrument by plucking or thumping the string. This instrument is

HOW TO MAKE A GUTBUCKET

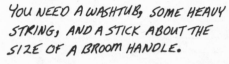

YOU NEED A WASHTUB, SOME HEAVY STRING, AND A STICK ABOUT THE SIZE OF A BROOM HANDLE.

WITH A BIG NAIL OR DRILL MAKE A HOLE IN THE CENTER OF THE BOTTOM OF YOUR TUB.

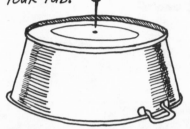

(PIECE OF WOOD OR WASHER) SO IT WON'T PULL THROUGH THE HOLE.

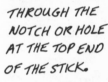

KNOT

SAW OR CARVE NOTCHES IN THE ENDS OF THE STICK.

AT ONE END (THE TOP) YOU CAN DRILL A HOLE INSTEAD OF THE NOTCH. LACE THE STRING OR WIRE THROUGH THE HOLE IN THE TUB. TIE A KNOT OR TIE THE STRING TO SOME OBJECT

SET THE NOTCHED END OF THE STICK ON THE TUB RIM. TIE THE STRING THROUGH THE NOTCH OR HOLE AT THE TOP END OF THE STICK.

THIS INSTRUMENT IS ABSOLUTELY WORTH-LESS UNLESS YOU PLAY IT SO PLAY!

COFFEE CAN BASS

COFFEE

BASS-IC BOX

EARTH-HARP

ALTERNATIVE BASSES

DRUM BASS

BUCKET BUCKET

HOME TUBS INC

great for playing along with other instruments, the radio, or records because you can alter the pitch quite rapidly. The trick is to match the tones of your instrument with the tones you are playing along with, or at least to make tones that sound good together. Listen carefully, it will all work out.

Checking Out Strings

The Greek mathematician Pythagoras (whom we can also thank for important discoveries in geometry) discovered in the sixth century B.C. that a vibrating string vibrates in sections.

To do his studies of the vibrating string, Pythagoras constructed an instrument called a monochord. Monochords are still used today by scientists and musicians. You can build one with a piece of wire, a board or a tabletop, some chunks of wood (for bridges), and a weight (bucket of sand makes a good one).

HOW TO MAKE A MONOCHORD

YOU NEED A PIECE OF WIRE 4 OR 5 FEET LONG, A BOARD ABOUT 3 FEET LONG, SOME CHUNKS OF WOOD FOR BRIDGES, AND A WEIGHT (A BUCKET OF SAND MAKES A GOOD ONE).

PUT A NAIL OR SCREW IN ONE END OF YOUR BOARD. TIE ONE END OF THE WIRE TO IT.

SET THE BRIDGES ON THE TOP OF THE BOARD NEAR THE ENDS. BRIDGES WORK BEST IF THEY HAVE A TRIANGULAR SHAPE SO THE STRING CONTACTS THEM AT ONLY ONE POINT.

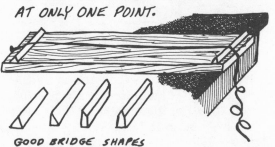

GOOD BRIDGE SHAPES

TIE THE BUCKET OF SAND OR ANOTHER WEIGHT TO THE DANGLING END OF THE WIRE. THE HANGING WEIGHT SHOULD PULL THE STRING TIGHT. YOUR MONOCHORD IS NOW READY TO PLAY.

YOU CAN MAKE A GOOD BUCKET BY PUNCHING TWO HOLES THROUGH A COFFEE CAN, THEN MAKING A WIRE HANDLE FOR IT.

More on Pitch and Strings

To play the monochord you can strike the string, stroke it with a bow, pluck it, or even blow on it between the bridges. When you have set the string in motion, you will hear a sound. While it is still sounding, push down on the weight. Notice that the pitch rises. The harder you press the weight, the higher the pitch rises.

Now leave the weight alone and move one of the bridges closer to the other. Pluck the string. The pitch is higher. Moving the bridges closer together shortens the vibrating part of the string. If the tension on the string remains the same, the pitch rises. If you move the bridges further apart, the pitch drops.

If you use the same weight and bridge positions but substitute a heavier or softer string, the pitch will become lower. With a thinner or harder string, the pitch will rise.

How Strings Vibrate

If you pluck the string of your monochord and watch it vibrate, it will probably look like a blur with this shape.

The blur is narrow at the ends and widest at the middle. Pluck the string again. This time watch it from one of the sides, then from the bottom, then from the top. Regardless of how you look at it, the shape of the vibrating string looks much the same. You can see that the string not only vibrates up and down, but also from side to side and around and around, all at the same time.

As you can see, the string vibrates along its total length. What you can't see is that it also vibrates in sections.

The blur you see is a result of the string's vibrating in many ways all at one time. A string vibrates in sections like this:

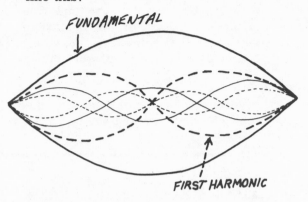

The pitch of the longest vibration of any given string is called the fundamental. Although the fundamental produces the main part of the sound, the secondary vibrations are also heard. These sounds are called harmonics, or overtones. If you hold your finger lightly on the string at the exact center between the bridges of your monochord and then pluck the string, you will hear

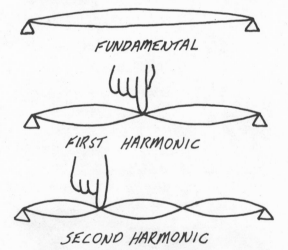

the first harmonic. The pitch of the first harmonic is twice as high as the pitch of the fundamental. By placing your finger on the center of the string you prevented it from moving at just the spot where it needs most to move to

30

produce the fundamental sound. As you can see from the diagram, the center of the string is a place where the first harmonic moves least. When you touch the string there, you do not interfere with the string's ability to produce the first harmonic vibration. If you have a tightly stretched steel string on your monochord, you can probably hear the second and third harmonics. Pluck as you place your finger at exactly one-third and one-fourth the length of the string.

A Boxful of Sound

Many musical instruments, especially stringed ones, have a sound box to make them louder. Sound boxes come in all sorts of shapes and sizes. They can be large and rectangular like the case of a piano or small and round like a coconut shell. Violins and guitars have sound boxes made of wood bent into curves. Some instruments have sound boxes made of clay bowls or gourds. The Russians have a family of guitarlike instruments called balalaikas that have triangle-shaped sound boxes. Almost all sound boxes have a top, a bottom, and sides—just like any other box.

The backs and sides of these boxes full of air are usually made of a hard material that bounces sound forward. The top of the box is called the sound-board. It is usually made of a thin sheet of wood or rawhide (sometimes metal, plastic, or cardboard is used). The vibrating strings shake the soundboard. Because it has a large flat surface, it can shake many more molecules of air than the vibrating string can by itself. When more molecules of air are vibrating, you hear a louder, richer sound. Somewhere in the soundboard of most stringed instruments there is a sound hole. The hole, or holes, connects the vibrating air inside the box with the air outside, which will carry the sound to your ears. Sound holes are sometimes drilled or sawed into shapes, so they also serve as decorations.

Because sound boxes are part of so many instruments, you may find that you'll want to make several of them. Each one may be slightly different, to follow the design of a different instrument. The instructions that follow are *general* rules for sound boxes; you can come back to them whenever a project calls for making one. Following the instructions for sound boxes, you'll find directions for making tuning pegs, another item that you'll be adding to several different instruments.

You can make your sound box as large or as small as you want. You should consider the materials you have, or can find, and also the kind and size of instrument you want to make.

31

HOW TO MAKE A SOUND BOX

CUT TWO PAIRS OF BOARDS FOR THE SIDES AND ENDS OF YOUR BOX.

FIRST CUT ONE PIECE THE LENGTH YOU WANT. THEN LAY THE PIECE YOU CUT ON TOP OF A LONGER PIECE. MATCH ONE END OF BOTH BOARDS. ——

MARK HERE, THEN SAW.

CUT A SECOND PAIR TO A LENGTH YOU WANT.

WITH ONE PAIR LYING FLAT SQUIRT GLUE ACROSS THEM NEAR THEIR ENDS. USE WHITE GLUE LIKE ELMER'S OR YELLOWISH CARPENTER'S GLUE

GLUE →

← GLUE

FIT THE GLUED ENDS TO THE ENDS OF THE UNGLUED PAIR TO FORM A RECTANGLE.

GLUE WORKS BETTER IF YOU CLAMP YOUR WORK.

BIG RUBBER BANDS OR STRIPS CUT FROM INNER TUBES ARE ESPECIALLY GOOD FOR CLAMPING BOXES. WRAP THE BAND AROUND THE SIDES. HAVE A FRIEND HELP HOLD YOUR WORK TO GET THE BAND STARTED.

THE SOUNDBOARD

FOR THE SOUNDBOARD (TOP) AND THE BOTTOM OF THE BOX YOU NEED A STRONG, THIN SHEET OF WOOD, 1/8-INCH PANELING, 1/4-INCH PLYWOOD, OR HEAVY CARDBOARD. THE SOUNDBOARD NEEDS TO BE AS THIN AS POSSIBLE, BUT STRONG ENOUGH TO SUPPORT THE TENSION OF THE STRINGS. DRILL OR SAW A SOUND HOLE IN THE SOUNDBOARD AND GLUE BRACES IF THEY ARE NECESSARY ON THE INSIDE SURFACE OF THE SOUNDBOARD **BEFORE** YOU GLUE IT ON THE BOX.

SQUIRT A LINE OF GLUE AROUND THE SIDE EDGES THEN SET THE BOTTOM ON THE SIDES.

GLUE ↓

FLIP OVER THE BOX. SQUIRT GLUE AROUND THE EDGES AND SET THE SOUNDBOARD ON IT.

CLAMP THE BACK AND SOUNDBOARD. USE "C" CLAMPS, A WEIGHT (BOOKS, BRICKS, ROCKS), OR RUBBER BANDS.

OTHER STYLES OF BOXING

EVERYONE WHO MIGHT WANT TO MAKE A STRINGED INSTRUMENT WITH A SOUND BOX MAY NOT HAVE THE MATERIALS OR TOOLS TO MAKE THE KIND SHOWN ON PAGE 32. DON'T DESPAIR, THERE ARE OTHER WAYS TO DO THE JOB. HERE ARE SOME OTHER WAYS AND THINGS PEOPLE USE TO MAKE MUSICAL INSTRUMENT SOUND BOXES.

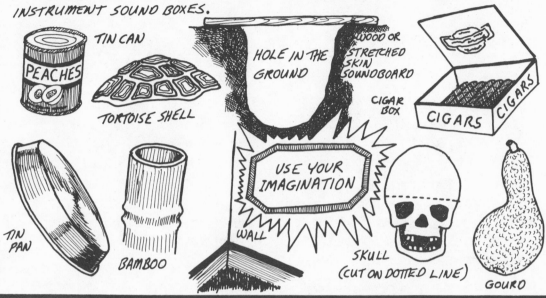

TIN CAN — PEACHES

TORTOISE SHELL

HOLE IN THE GROUND

WOOD OR STRETCHED SKIN SOUNDBOARD

CIGAR BOX — CIGARS CIGARS

USE YOUR IMAGINATION

TIN PAN

BAMBOO

WALL

SKULL (CUT ON DOTTED LINE)

GOURD

Tuning Pegs

Tuning pegs are the most common device for tuning a stringed instrument. Because the string is attached to the peg, the musician can raise or lower the string's pitch by turning it. You may want to look back to the discussion on page 30. With wood, a drill, a coping saw, a file, or a pocket knife and a little care you can make pegs much like those on a violin.

Lyre, Lyre

The lyre was a popular, ancient musical instrument. Lyres were very popular with the ancient Greeks. According to Greek legend, Hermes, messenger of the gods, was said to have made the first lyra (a type of lyre with a tortoise-shell sound box) from a tor-toise shell he found in Egypt. Greek amateur musicians played the lyra while the professionals played a lyre with a box-shaped sound box called the kithara. They used their lyres to accompany songs and recitations of poems and stories. King David, the king of Israel, was a lyre player. So was the Roman god Apollo.

TUNING PEGS

DECIDE WHERE YOU WANT TO PLACE THE PEGS. THEN DRILL A HOLE FOR EACH PEG. THEY SHOULD BE AT LEAST 1/4 INCH IN DIAMETER

TAPER THE HOLE. THE MOST EFFECTIVE WAY TO TAPER A HOLE FOR TUNING PEGS IS TO USE A RAT-TAIL FILE IN A DRILL. IF YOU USE AN ELECTRIC DRILL, YOU MUST USE A REVERSIBLE ONE THAT GOES BACK-WARDS OR THE FILE WILL GET STUCK.

YOU CAN ALSO TWIST THE TAPERED HANDLE END OF A FILE IN THE HOLE TO TAPER IT.

FILE

BEFORE   DURING   AFTER

WITH A COPING SAW YOU CAN CUT SOME ROUGH SHAPES OUT OF A BOARD. HERE ARE SOME POSSIBLE SHAPES.

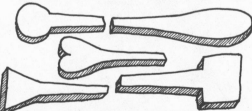

WITH A FILE OR A POCKET KNIFE ROUND THE SHAFTS OF THE PEGS TO FIT YOUR TAPERED HOLES. SQUEEZE THE PEG INTO THE HOLE AND TWIST IT A LITTLE. A SHINY SPOT WILL

FORM WHERE THE PEG NEEDS TO BE TRIMMED OR FILED MORE. SAND THE PEGS TO MAKE THEM SMOOTH.

DRILL A SMALL HOLE THROUGH THE SHAFT TO KEEP THE STRING FROM SLIPPING.

IF YOUR PEGS SLIP, PUT POWDERED ROSIN IN THE HOLE OR ON THE SHAFT TO INCREASE THEIR FRICTION. PULL THE PEG OUT TO TURN.

OUT   IN   PUSH IN TO GRIP.

PEG OPTIONS:

BRASS SCREW WITH A HOLE DRILLED IN IT.

TAPERED WOOD DOWEL WITH A NAIL THROUGH IT FOR A HANDLE.

EYE SCREW

IF YOU USE SCREWS, YOU MUST START THE SCREWS INTO THE WOOD BEFORE STRETCHING STRINGS TO THEM. STRETCH THE STRING TIGHT BEFORE TYING IT AT THE SCREW.

YOU CAN TIGHTEN EYE SCREWS BY USING A NAIL THROUGH THE LOOP FOR A HANDLE.

HOW TO MAKE A LYRE

YOU NEED SOME STRINGS, THREE PIECES OF WOOD ABOUT 2 FEET LONG (BRANCHES AN INCH OR SO THICK OR 1"x2" BOARDS ARE GOOD), AND A SOUND BOX (A PLASTIC BLEACH BOTTLE WORKS).

TIE THE THREE STICKS TOGETHER TO FORM A TRIANGLE. WRAP AND TIE THE JOINTS TIGHT SO THE STICKS WON'T SLIDE. YOU CAN ALSO HAMMER A NAIL IN THE JOINTS FOR GOOD MEASURE.

ATTACH THE SOUND BOX TO THE FRAME BY: POKING OR DRILLING HOLES THROUGH THE SOUND BOX FOR THE FRAME TO FIT THROUGH.

TIE IT SECURELY IN ONE OF THE ANGLES OF THE FRAME. IF YOUR SOUND BOX IS THIN, YOU CAN SET IT ON TOP OF THE FRAME.

YOU COULD ALSO BUILD THE SOUND BOX AND FRAME AS ONE UNIT.

THE NEXT STEP IS TO TIE THE STRINGS TO THE ANGLE BELOW THE SOUND BOX. MONOFILAMENT FISHING LINE, WIRE, OR STRONG STRING SOUNDS GOOD. THEN STRETCH THE STRINGS TO THE CROSSBAR.

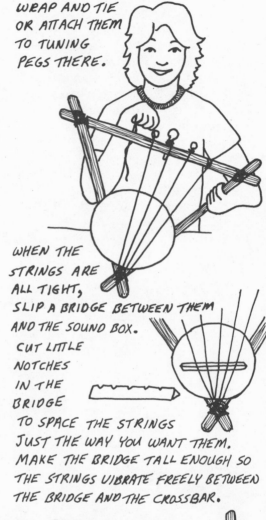

WRAP AND TIE OR ATTACH THEM TO TUNING PEGS THERE.

WHEN THE STRINGS ARE ALL TIGHT, SLIP A BRIDGE BETWEEN THEM AND THE SOUND BOX. CUT LITTLE NOTCHES IN THE BRIDGE TO SPACE THE STRINGS JUST THE WAY YOU WANT THEM. MAKE THE BRIDGE TALL ENOUGH SO THE STRINGS VIBRATE FREELY BETWEEN THE BRIDGE AND THE CROSSBAR.

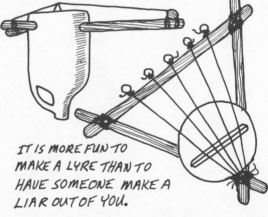

IT IS MORE FUN TO MAKE A LYRE THAN TO HAVE SOMEONE MAKE A LIAR OUT OF YOU.

The minstrels of medieval Europe also accompanied their songs on lyres, but since that time, the popularity of lyres has faded. Today they are played mainly in the African countries of Kenya, Uganda, Ethiopia, and Sudan. The obukano of Kenya is a very large lyre with a wooden-bow sound box and eight strings. The soundboard is made of a stretched animal skin.

Lyres consist of a sound box with two arms branching upward from the sides. Near the top of the arms, the arms are fastened to a crossbar. Strings run from the bottom of the sound box across a bridge on the soundboard and are tied or attached to tuning pegs or rings on the crossbar. There are generally 7 strings on a lyre, but sometimes as many as 18 or 20.

The lyre is held between the player's knees, and its strings are plucked with a plectrum, or pick, made of ivory or hardwood. The plectrum is held in the right hand. The fingers of the left hand pluck the strings from the other side of the instrument.

Sounds Like Heaven

On harps, the instruments that angels are rumored to play, the strings run at an angle from the soundboard to the neck. Each string on a harp produces one note when it is plucked by the player's fingers. Its sound is gentle and silvery, and often harps are used to create misty, mysterious, or dreamy moods in music. They are seldom used as a melody instrument in European music. Though mostly used for quiet music, harps are also used to play lively tunes. Lively harp music is especially popular in the Andes mountains of South America.

There are three basic types of harps. A musical bow equipped with a sound box and several strings is one type. It is

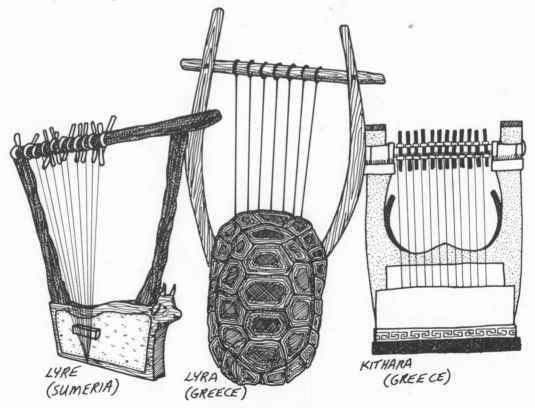

LYRE
(SUMERIA)

LYRA
(GREECE)

KITHARA
(GREECE)

36

called a bow harp. The harps in which the neck and the sound box meet to form an angle are called, cleverly enough, angle harps. Frame harps are the third type. They look like angle harps with a support connecting the neck and the sound box at their non-common end. They are usually triangular in shape.

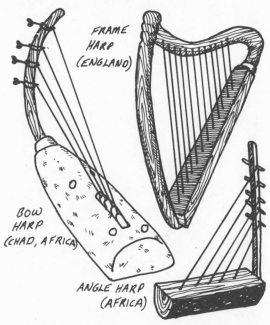

FRAME HARP (ENGLAND)

BOW HARP (CHAD, AFRICA)

ANGLE HARP (AFRICA)

The earliest harps were probably musical bows with several strings and a sound box. They were known in Egypt and Sumeria as early as 3000 B. C. Angle harps were a later development and probably came from Persia. They make appearances in Egyptian art dating from about 2000 B.C. Frame harps were developed during the Middle Ages. Whether these harps were developed by the Vikings, Irish, Welsh, or Dutch nobody knows for sure. The first frame harps were small, portable, and sturdy.

Over many years the large orchestral harp evolved from those ancestors. The orchestral harp, which stands about 6 feet high, is now a regular instrument of the symphony orchestra. It has the largest range of pitches of all the instruments in the orchestra. The player plucks the strings with his or her fingers to make them sound. The harpist actually pulls the string and releases it—a little like shooting a bow and arrow—when she plucks. Pedals on the harp raise the pitch of the strings so that three separate pitches can be played on each string.

Small frame harps are played by folk musicians in South America and the British Isles. People in Ireland especially enjoy the music of the harp, and one of Ireland's national symbols is the harp, a symbol of harmony. Bow harps are popular folk instruments in the African countries of Uganda, Liberia, Tanzania, Zaire, and Chad, and in some Asian countries. Angle harps are also common in Africa.

HOW TO MAKE A HARP

YOU CAN MAKE A BOW HARP BY ADDING A SOUND BOX, SEVERAL STRINGS, AND TUNING PEGS (IF YOU LIKE) TO A BOWED STICK AT LEAST 1 INCH THICK.

YOU NEED TO BUILD OR FIND A SOUND BOX. TIN CANS OR PLASTIC BOTTLES ARE GOOD. IF YOU BUILD ONE, LEAVE THE BOTTOM OFF AND DRILL HOLES IN THE ENDS LARGE ENOUGH FOR YOUR BOWED STICK TO FIT THROUGH.

GLUE

GLUE A REINFORCING STRIP OF WOOD ON THE INNER SIDE OF THE SOUNDBOARD. PUT IT IN THE CENTER RUNNING LENGTHWISE.

DRILL A ROW OF VERY SMALL HOLES, JUST BIG ENOUGH FOR THE STRINGS YOU ARE GOING TO PUT THROUGH THEM. DRILL THE HOLES THROUGH THE SOUNDBOARD AND REINFORCING STRIP.

LACE THE STRINGS THROUGH THE HOLES. KNOTS ON THE UNDER SIDE KEEP THEM FROM PULLING THROUGH.

KNOTS

PUT A NAIL HERE OR WRAP WITH STRING.

SLIP THE BOW THROUGH THE HOLES IN THE ENDS OF THE BOX. TO KEEP THE BOX FROM SLIDING ON THE BOW WRAP THE BOW WITH STRING OR HAMMER A NAIL IN IT.

STRETCH THE STRINGS TIGHT FROM THE SOUNDBOARD TO THE BOW.

YOU CAN DRILL HOLES OR CUT NOTCHES TO KEEP THE STRINGS FROM SLIPPING DOWN THE BOW.

YOU CAN MAKE TUNING PEGS OR SCREWS TO TUNE YOUR HARP.

VIEW OF BOTTOM

FOR A LOUDER HARP COVER THE BACK OF THE SOUND BOX. LEAVE A SLIT SO YOU CAN CHANGE STRINGS WHEN THEY BREAK.

YOU CAN MAKE AN ANGLE HARP FROM A STRONG FORKED BRANCH OR A FRAME HARP BY ADDING A SOUND BOX AND STRINGS TO A TRIANGULAR FRAME.

ANGLE FOR A HARP

TWO-CAN HARP

Caught by the Neck
of the Lute

Lutes are native to all parts of the world and come in so many shapes and sizes that entire books are printed about just them. Of all the stringed instruments they seem to be the most lovable. Instruments like the guitar, mandolin, and banjo belong to the lute family. The violin and its relatives are also lutes, but because they are played by rubbing the strings with a bow, they form a separate division of the family. They are called fiddles.

Lutes have a resonating body with a neck attached. They have strings that run from near the base of the body along the full length of the neck. The neck of the instrument allows the player to stop the strings with his or her fingers. Remember that the

shorter a vibrating string is, the higher its pitch will be. The lengths of their necks, sizes and shapes of their bodies, kinds of strings, and the presence or absence of frets are some of the ways lutes differ from one another.

Many lutes have fretted necks. This kind of fret doesn't mean there is something to worry about. Frets, in fact, take some of the worry out of placing your fingers on the string in just the right place. Frets are little bars of wood, cord, or metal that run across the neck and stick up above it. They are spaced the proper distance apart so that when a string is pushed against them its vibrating length is shortened just the right amount for a particular tone. Then when the player plucks the string with his other hand, that particular tone will sound. Without the help of frets the player has to place his or

PARTS OF A LUTE
(NEAPOLITAN MANDOLIN)

PEG HEAD

TUNING PEGS

NUT

FRETS

NECK

SOUND HOLE

ROSETTE

BRIDGE

STRINGS

BACK OR SOUND BOX

TAILPIECE

SOUNDBOARD

her fingers very accurately in order to play the correct tone. Now that's something to fret about!

The sound boxes, or bodies of lutes may be made of wood, gourds, clay, metal, or plastics. They act as resonating chambers for vibrations of the strings. When they are made of a thin, hard material they work best.

The shape of the lute body affects the sound the instrument can make. If the body is very small, the higher pitched sounds are stronger. If the body is large, the slower, lower vibrations have more chance of expressing themselves. Bodies with curved insides reflect sound well. Those with square corners tend to absorb more of the sound energy and keep it from being heard.

HI-FA-LUTE-N

BLEACHBOTTLE BANJO

TINPAN GUITAR

SOME LUTES FROM AROUND THE WORLD

BLUEGRASS MANDOLIN (USA)

RAMKIE (SOUTH AFRICA)

SAMISEN (JAPAN)

TAR (TURKEY)

Most of the discoveries about lute shapes, sizes, and materials were made by trial and error. The places where the instrument makers lived and the materials available have influenced these choices. Over many centuries some beautiful, weird, amazing lutes have been built and played. Some of the finest ideas were developed before science had progressed enough to be of much help, but with and without science, lute makers are always trying to come up with better-sounding instruments.

Something to Fret About

To put frets on your lute in the right places you use a rule called "the rule of eighteenths." The first fret, measuring from the nut, is placed at a distance of 1/18 the length of the string from the bridge to the nut. The second fret is located 1/18 the distance from the first fret to the bridge. The third fret is placed 1/18 the distance from the second fret to the bridge. You can go on down the neck this way to add as many

frets as you want on the neck of your instrument.

Frets need to be placed in just the right spot, so measure carefully. A precise way to measure for them is to make a fret scale. Instructions for drawing a fret scale are on page 43.

An Old Favorite

The guitar is a plucked lute with a body shaped like a fat "8." It has a large round hole in the middle of the soundboard. The back and soundboard are normally flat and made of wood. Spruce is the preferred wood for soundboards. The curved sides and the back of the body are made from dense hardwood to deflect the sound. Brazilian rosewood is often used for these parts. Other hardwoods such as cypress, maple, and mahogany are also used for the sides and backs of fine instruments.

The guitar has a fretted fingerboard on its neck. A peg head tops the neck. Six strings are attached to the tuning pegs in the peg head. The other ends of

HOW TO MAKE A LUTE

TO MAKE A LUTE YOU NEED A BOARD FOR THE NECK, SOUND BOX, STRINGS, TUNING PEGS OR SCREWS, NAILS, GLUE, A HAMMER, SAW, AND A DRILL. A 1" X 2" BOARD MAKES A GOOD NECK. CUT A PIECE THAT IS 4 INCHES LONGER THAN YOUR SOUND BOX. PUT AN "A" ON THIS PIECE.

CUT ANOTHER PIECE ABOUT 18 INCHES LONG. MARK "B" ON IT. THIS IS THE NECK.

SAW, DRILL, OR CUT HOLES IN THE ENDS OF YOUR SOUND BOX THAT BOARD "A" WILL FIT THROUGH SNUGGLY. THE TOP EDGE OF THE HOLES SHOULD BE AS FAR FROM THE SOUNDBOARD AS THE NECK IS THICK.

PUT GLUE ON A 3-INCH LENGTH OF BOARD "A." SET "B" ON "A" WITH THE GLUE BETWEEN THEM.

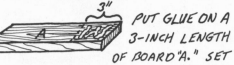

NAIL "B" TO "A."

GLUE — NAILS

TOP VIEW

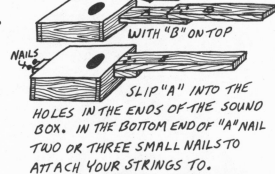

WITH "B" ON TOP

NAILS

SLIP "A" INTO THE HOLES IN THE ENDS OF THE SOUND BOX. IN THE BOTTOM END OF "A" NAIL TWO OR THREE SMALL NAILS TO ATTACH YOUR STRINGS TO.

DRILL HOLES FOR TUNING PEGS OR START EYE SCREWS AT THE TOP OF "B." SCREWS WORK BEST IF YOU PUT THEM IN THE END OF THE BOARD. TIE THE STRINGS ON THE NAILS IN THE END OF "A" AND STRETCH THEM AS TIGHT AS YOU CAN TO THE TUNING PEGS OR SCREWS.

BRIDGE →   MAKE THE NUT AND BRIDGE FROM SMALL PIECES OF WOOD. MAKE NOTCHES TO SPACE THE STRINGS.   ← NUT

INSERT THE NUT BETWEEN THE STRINGS AND NECK JUST BELOW THE PEGS. INSERT THE BRIDGE BETWEEN THE STRINGS AND THE SOUNDBOARD. THE BRIDGE AND NUT LIFT THE STRINGS SO THEY CAN VIBRATE FREELY. CUT NOTCHES IN THEM TO SPACE THE STRINGS JUST THE WAY YOU WANT THEM. THE BRIDGE CARRIES THE VIBRATIONS FROM THE STRINGS TO THE SOUND-BOARD.

DRAWING A FRET SCALE

TO MAKE A SCALE TO MEASURE FRETS YOU NEED A LONG PIECE OF PAPER, A COMPASS, A PROTRACTOR,

2 SHARP PENCILS, AND A YARDSTICK.

MEASURE THE DISTANCE FROM THE NUT TO THE BRIDGE ON YOUR LUTE. THIS LENGTH IS THE "VIBRATING STRING LENGTH"(VSL).

IF THE VSL IS EASILY DIVIDED BY 18 - SAY 18, 22, OR 27 INCHES - IT WILL BE EASIER TO FIGURE. FOR THIS EXAMPLE WE WILL USE 18 INCHES.

DRAW A STRAIGHT LINE 18 INCHES LONG ON YOUR PAPER. WITH THE PROTRACTOR AND YOUR PENCIL DRAW A LINE PERPENDICULAR TO THE VSL (18") LINE AS SHOWN.

DIVIDE 18 INTO THE LENGTH OF THE VSL (18") AND YOU GET 1". MEASURE THIS DISTANCE ON THE LINE PERPENDICULAR TO THE VSL LINE.

$$18\overline{)18''}\;{}^{1''}$$

DRAW A DIAGONAL FROM THE POINT

ON THE PERPENDICULAR TO THE OTHER END OF THE 18" LINE.

SET THE COMPASS SO ITS METAL POINT IS AT THE POINT WHERE THE PERPENDICULAR LINES MEET AND THE PENCIL POINT IS AT THE POINT WHERE THE DIAGONAL CROSSES THE SHORT LINE. MAKE AN ARC WITH THE COMPASS THAT CROSSES THE 18" LINE.

WHERE THE ARC CROSSES THE VSL LINE DRAW A LINE PERPENDICULAR TO IT. ADJUST THE COMPASS TO THE NEW (SHORTER) DISTANCE BETWEEN THE 18" LINE AND THE DIAGONAL AND DRAW A NEW ARC.

CONTINUE THIS PROCEDURE DOWN THE LINE. THE POINTS WHERE ARCS INTERSECT THE VSL LINE ARE WHERE THE FRETS BELONG. MARK YOUR LUTE - NOTICE THAT THE FRETS ARE FURTHEST APART NEAR THE NUT.

FOR FRETS YOU CAN GLUE ON TOOTHPICKS OR WRAP STRING OR RUBBER BANDS AROUND THE NECK. TWELVE FRETS WILL ALLOW YOU TO PLAY A MAJOR SCALE ON ONE STRING.

the strings are attached to the bridge, which is glued onto the soundboard.

The wood of the guitar body is thin so it will project and amplify sound energy instead of absorbing it. To make it rigid it is braced inside with thin struts of wood. The struts under the soundboard are especially important. They must make the soundboard strong enough to withstand the tension of the stretched strings but also allow it to vibrate and amplify the vibrations of the strings.

The method of bracing used in most classical guitars is called fan bracing. It was developed by a Spanish guitarmaker, Antonio de Torres-Jurado, in about 1850. Torres is credited with inventing the guitar as we know it today. Guitarmakers continue to search for better methods of bracing and making instruments, but Torres's method is still the most widely used.

The guitar has moved in and out of popularity through its long history. There have been times when it was regarded as an inferior instrument. But

today it enjoys a wide range of enthusiastic friends. Guitars are easy to love. They are a comfortable size and easy to learn to play. They have a warm, wide range of tone, a gentle spirit, and

LOOKING INSIDE A GUITAR

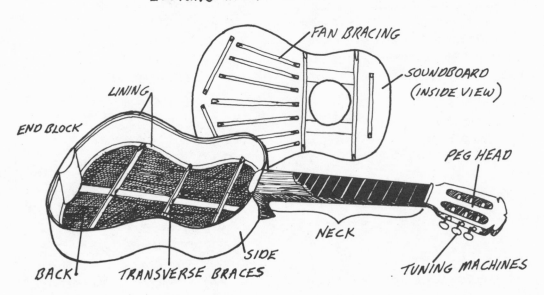

FAN BRACING

SOUNDBOARD (INSIDE VIEW)

LINING

END BLOCK

PEG HEAD

NECK

BACK

TRANSVERSE BRACES

SIDE

TUNING MACHINES

are suitable for use in many types of music. Classical soloists play intricate compositions while many other musicians use guitars to accompany singing or other instruments.

The steel string guitar is a rather recent development. It has a louder sound that suits some performers well. Because the tension on the steel strings is great, these guitars have heavier bracing than classical guitars, which have nylon strings. They are made in different styles for playing different kinds of music. Some even have 12 strings instead of 6. Others are fitted with electronic equipment, which amplifies and can change the vibrations of the strings to produce special sound effects.

Hey Fiddle, Fiddle

When lutes are made to be played with a bow, they are called fiddles. The bow is rubbed across the strings, causing them to vibrate.

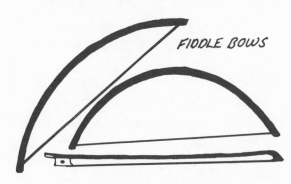

FIDDLE BOWS

The bow consists of a stick and a string or bunch of hair that is treated with rosin to increase its friction against the strings of the fiddle. Bows are haired with silk strands in China and Japan. Some in Africa have cords of plant fibers. The violin bow is strung with horsehair from white horses, while the bows used to play cellos and double basses are sometimes haired

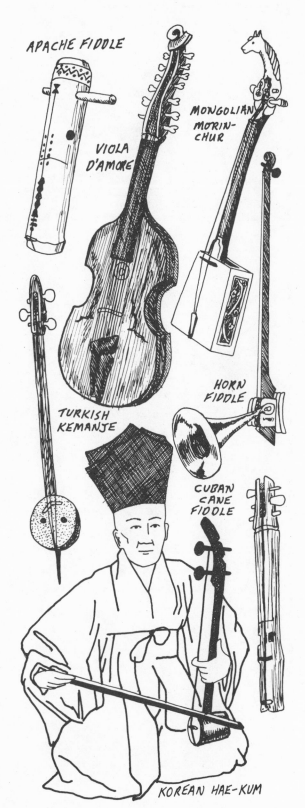

APACHE FIDDLE

VIOLA D'AMORE

MONGOLIAN MORIN-CHUR

TURKISH KEMANJE

HORN FIDDLE

CUBAN CANE FIDDLE

KOREAN HAE-KUM

45

HOW TO MAKE A SPIKE FIDDLE

YOU NEED A TIN CAN, A STRAIGHT STICK (ABOUT 2 FEET LONG), AND SOME STRING. WIRE OR MONOFILAMENT LINE WORKS BEST.

WITH A COLD CHISEL AND A HAMMER MAKE HOLES LARGE ENOUGH FOR THE STICK TO GO THROUGH THE CAN.

BEND IN THE FLAPS WITH PLIERS. JAGGED TIN EDGES CAN CUT. WEAR GLOVES FOR SAFETY.

PUSH THE STICK THROUGH THE HOLES SO AN INCH STICKS OUT ONE SIDE AND THE OTHER END IS 1 OR 2 FEET LONG. WRAP THE STICK WITH STRING SO THE CAN WON'T SLIDE ALONG IT.

MOST SPIKE FIDDLES HAVE THREE OR FEWER STRINGS. TIE ONE END OF THE STRINGS TO THE SHORT END OF THE STICK, THEN STRETCH THEM OVER THE SOUNDBOARD END OF THE CAN. PULL THE STRINGS TIGHT AND TIE THEM EITHER THROUGH A NOTCH IN THE END OF THE STICK, TO A PEG, OR TO AN EYE SCREW.

SPIKE FIDDLES OFTEN HAVE A MOVABLE NUT. YOU CAN USE IT TO HELP TUNE THE STRING(S).

NUT

BRIDGE

WHEN YOU SLIDE THE NUT UP OR DOWN THE NECK, THE PITCH CHANGES.

INSERT THE BRIDGE (A WEDGE OF WOOD, SHORT STICK, SEASHELL, OR STONE) BETWEEN THE SOUNDBOARD AND STRING.

TO PLAY A FIDDLE YOU NEED A BOW. MAKE A MUSICAL BOW, PAGE 24, BUT USE A STRIP OF CLOTH ABOUT AN INCH WIDE FOLDED OVER TWICE, A HEAVY COTTON STRING, OR A SMALL BUNCH OF LIGHTER STRINGS FOR THE "HAIR" ON YOUR BOW.

ROSIN

RUB ROSIN ON THE CLOTH STRIP OR STRING OF THE BOW TO INCREASE ITS FRICTION.

with black horsehair, which is rougher and vibrates their heavy strings better.

You can make a fiddle bow by putting rosin on a cotton string and tying it across a bowed wooden stick. Rosin is necessary equipment for fiddle players. It comes in a chunk and looks like amber glass. You can buy it at a music store or sometimes at a hardware store. It is made from the sap of pine trees.

A fiddle string vibrates at the same pitch when it is bowed as when it is plucked. Using the bow allows the musician to make continuous tones, and by moving the bow back and forth across the string the musician provides a steady supply of energy to the string.

Vibrations from the string travel through the bridge to the soundboard and body of the fiddle. Those parts set the surrounding air and the air inside into motion. The vibrations travel through the air to reach your ear.

Wood is the most common material for the bodies and soundboards of fiddles. But bodies are also made from gourds, bamboo, coconut shells, clay, and metal. Some fiddle soundboards are made from stretched animal hides.

Fiddles are so popular that they've made their way into lots of stories and nursery rhymes. Remember what Old King Cole called for? And, of course, there was that cat when the cow jumped over the moon.

A TIME FOR FIDDLIN' AROUND

HOLD YOUR FIDDLE UPRIGHT WITH THE SOUND BOX RESTING ON YOUR LAP. WITH ONE HAND SLIDE THE "HAIR" OF THE BOW ACROSS THE FIDDLE STRING(S) JUST A FEW INCHES UP FROM THE BRIDGE. WITH YOUR OTHER HAND YOU CAN CHANGE THE PITCH OF THE STRING(S) AS YOU PLAY. MOVE YOUR FINGERS UP AND DOWN THE STRING(S) LIKE A SPIDER ON A WALK. NOTICE HOW THE PITCH CHANGES. WITH PRACTICE YOU CAN PRODUCE THE EXACT TONES YOU WANT TO PLAY. THINK THE TONE YOU WANT AND MATCH THE SOUND YOU ARE MAKING TO IT.

IF EVER THERE WAS A TIME FOR FIDDLING AROUND, THIS IS IT.

WHEN HE WAS 62, OTTO E. FUNK WALKED 4,165 MILES FROM NEW YORK TO SAN FRANCISCO, PLAYING HIS VIOLIN EVERY STEP OF THE WAY. THE TRIP TOOK 183 DAYS. NOW THAT'S FIDDLING AROUND!

The Fancy Fiddle Family
of the Symphony

More than half the members of the symphony orchestra play fiddles. These instruments are all members of the violin family, which includes violins, violas, cellos, and the double basses. This family evolved from earlier fiddles in the sixteenth century. They differ from their ancestors a little in shape and size, but most noticeably in tone and strength of sound. Most are held differently now for playing than their ancestors were.

The violin was developed around 1550. One of the first people to make this wonderful fiddle was Andrea Amati. His sons were also violin-makers, and his grandson, Nicolo Amati, became the greatest violin-maker in the family. His instruments are known for their sweet tone. He taught many students to make violins, including Antonio Stradivari.

Stradivari lived in Cremona, Italy, where he worked for Amati for many years until he was able to open his own shop in about 1680. For several years he continued to make instruments after Amati's designs. But instrument makers are always looking for ways to make their instruments better sounding, and Stradivari began to make modifications and improvements. In his hands the development of the violin reached a high point. His greatest instruments were made after 1707 until his death in 1737. He made about 1,200 violins, violas, and cellos during his life.

Some fine examples of his work still survive and are played by musical artists. His best instruments have great power and beautiful tone. They are easy to play and are considered by many musicians to be the finest violins in existence. Stradivari instruments are greatly treasured and sell today for hundreds of thousands of dollars.

The violin is the smallest member of its family. Its soundboard is carved, usually from a piece of silver spruce, and swells up toward the center. The back of the instrument swells out in the opposite direction. The body has a curve or hollow on each side about half way up its length. This "waist" gives the musician room to move his or her bow back and forth across the four strings of the instrument. The back and sides of a violin are usually made of maple wood. Inside the hollow of the body under one foot of the bridge a small round stick called the soundpost is fitted. It carries vibrations from the bridge to the back of the instrument.

The violin is held between the player's chin and shoulder as it is bowed to make music. The fingerboard does not have frets, so the musician must feel and listen to play the correct tone. Many sound effects can be produced on the violin by different movements and pressures on the bow.

The next bigger member of the violin family is the viola. It looks like a violin and is played under the chin, but it is larger. If the violin is a soprano, the viola plays the alto part. It has a beautiful tone that is deeper and more resonant than the violin. Like the other members of its family, the viola has a soundboard with two "f" holes that connect the air inside the instrument to the air outside it. During this century the viola has become recognized more widely as a rich, expressive solo instrument.

The cello has a grand, deep tone. It is far too big in size to be played under the chin so it is held between the knees of the seated player. It stands on the floor on a single leg called a tail pin. The long thick strings of the cello are tuned one octave below (and they vibrate half as fast as) the strings of the viola. The cello is able to play bass parts because of its thick strings and large resonating body. It is a beautiful baritone-melody instrument.

The double bass is even larger than the cello. The musician who plays it must either stand or sit on a tall stool. Its lowest notes are even lower than those of the tuba. Basses, as they are often called, can be either plucked or bowed. They help set the beat in jazz as well as in the orchestra. In the hands of fine musicians they can also be exciting solo instruments.

Instruments of the violin family can be made in different sizes. A child can learn to play on a very small violin when he or she is small. As the child grows, he or she can change to a larger version of the same instrument. Some children start learning to play the violin when they are only three years old.

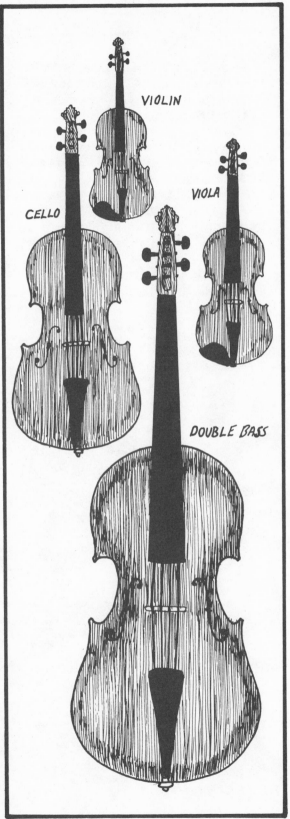

VIOLIN

VIOLA

CELLO

DOUBLE BASS

Z Is for Zither

When stringed instruments have their strings parallel to the body and the strings stretch from one end of the body to the other, the instruments are zithers. This group ranges from tube zithers, made of a single bamboo tube, to the piano with its many strings and tons of tension.

The simplest of the zithers is undoubtedly the ground zither. It is made by digging a hole in the ground and laying a thin board over it. A forked branch is set on the board, fork end up, and a string is stretched from a stake pounded in the ground on one side of the hole, through the fork of the stick, and tied to a second stake on the opposite side of the hole. To play the instrument the string is tapped with a stick. The hole in the ground acts as a resonator. Ground zithers are native to parts of Africa, but you can build one anywhere you can dig a hole.

Tube zithers are usually made from bamboo tubes. A string is cut from the fibers of one side of the tube. Between the tube and the string, bridges are inserted at each end. The bridges allow the string to vibrate freely and also stretch it. Valihas are tube zithers played in Malagasy. They have strings made of a material other than the tube

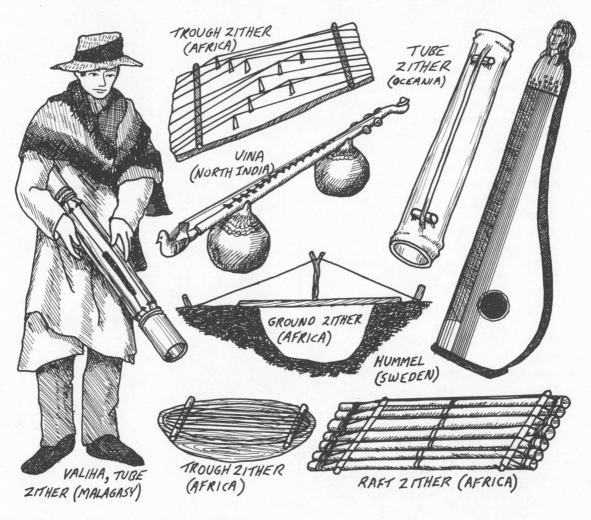

TROUGH ZITHER (AFRICA)

TUBE ZITHER (OCEANIA)

VINA (NORTH INDIA)

GROUND ZITHER (AFRICA)

HUMMEL (SWEDEN)

VALIHA, TUBE ZITHER (MALAGASY)

TROUGH ZITHER (AFRICA)

RAFT ZITHER (AFRICA)

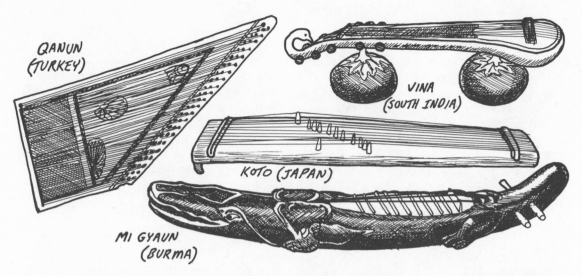

QANUN
(TURKEY)

VINA
(SOUTH INDIA)

KOTO (JAPAN)

MI GYAUN
(BURMA)

of bamboo and a slit-shaped sound hole. Some have tuning pegs to tune the strings. Tube zithers played in Yugoslavia are bowed rather than plucked. When several tube zithers are tied together side by side they form a raft zither.

Trough zithers have their strings stretched over a flat board with sticks or bridges to hold the string so it can vibrate. Some are made by stretching strings across a bowl.

In the Far East long zithers are common. The koto of Japan, ch'in of China, and the kayakeum of Korea are long zithers. The kayakeum and koto have movable bridges. To tune the silk strings to play different scales the musician slides the bridges along the soundboard and changes the vibrating length of the strings. Music of the Orient is written in many different scales, so the movable bridges are necessary.

One of the most important stringed instruments in India is a stick zither called the vina. A stick along which the strings are stretched and fingered is set on two gourds that serve as resonators. Vinas come in several styles—the width of the neck can vary, some have frets, others are unfretted.

Board zithers are common in Europe. They have a flat sound box that is often triangular or a trapezoid shape. The instrument is held in the arms or on the lap while the strings are plucked with the fingers or a plectrum.

The Appalachian dulcimore, Norwegian lanleik, Icelandic lanfspil, Hawaiian electric steel guitar, and Swedish hummel are board zithers with a little bit of lute blood. Each has a fretted fingerboard under a few of its strings. The melody and some chords are played on the fretted strings. The unfretted strings are called drones. Each produces only a single tone.

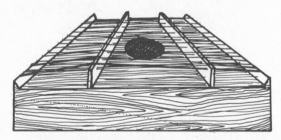

HAMMERED DULCIMER

A breeze plays the aeolian harp, another board zither. It has a long, narrow sound box that is fitted into a windowsill. When the window is opened just a little above the strings, the breeze blowing through the crack makes the strings vibrate. The aeolian harp plays a soft whistling music.

51

Another zither called a harp is the autoharp. It is a strummed board zither set up with keys. The keys have felt pads under them. The pads are arranged so that when the key is pressed, they muffle the sound of all the strings that are not part of the desired chord. The autoharp is played by folk singers to accompany their songs. The strings can also be plucked individually with a plectrum.

Dulcimers are board zithers that are played with little hammers or beaters held in the musician's hands. When the strings are struck they begin to vibrate. These instruments developed first in the Middle East, then in Europe, and much later in the Orient. The Persian santir, Russian chang, Hungarian cymbalom, and Chinese yang chin, or butterfly harp, are dulcimers. If you say the words "chang, cymbalom, yang chin," or, better yet, sing

them, you can get an idea of how a hammered dulcimer sounds. (All languages use onomatopoeia.) The hammers with which they are hit are light and bouncy and so is the tone of the hammered dulcimer.

The piano, harpsichord, and clavichord are widely known keyboard zithers. In each of these instruments the musician taps a key to make the strings sound. Each works in a unique way.

Pressing the keys of the harpsichord causes a small plectrum to pluck the string and set it into vibration. The first harpsichords were made in Italy in the 1500s. The instrument became popular and spread over Europe. Its quiet tinkling sound was an important part of the music of the baroque period (around 1600 to 1750). Virginals and spinets are smaller than the harpsichord but are sounded by the same plucking action.

The clavichord was also popular in the baroque period. When its keys are pressed, a small brass blade called a tangent hits the string to make it vibrate. The tangent also acts like a bridge that divides the string into two vibrating lengths. One length does not produce a sound because it is muffled by a damper.

Finally we get to the instrument found in schools and homes that children love to practice! The piano—also called the pianoforte—has felt hammers that strike the strings when the keys are pressed. The first piano was built by an Italian instrument maker named Bartolommeo Cristofori around 1700. It did not stir much interest in Italy, but an article written about it was translated into German. The article is believed to have inspired a German instrument maker, Gottfried Silbermann, to start making pianos. One of Silbermann's students then took

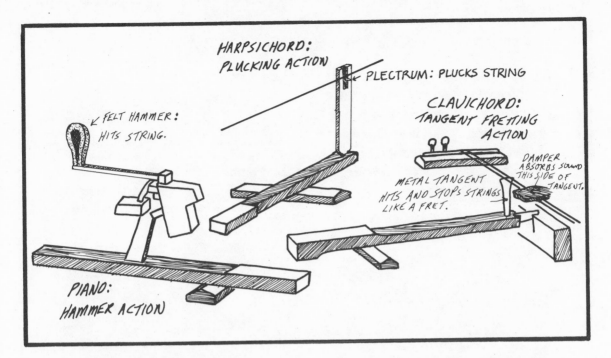

HARPSICHORD:
PLUCKING ACTION

PLECTRUM: PLUCKS STRING

CLAVICHORD:
TANGENT FRETTING
ACTION

FELT HAMMER:
HITS STRING.

DAMPER
ABSORBS SOUND
THIS SIDE OF
TANGENT.

METAL TANGENT
HITS AND STOPS STRINGS
LIKE A FRET.

PIANO:
HAMMER ACTION

piano making to England, and the craft spread and developed over the next several hundred years.

The first pianos had all wooden frames, but these were replaced by cast iron frames, which are stronger. A strong frame is needed in a piano because the stretched strings create a strain of up to 17 tons of pressure! Behind the frame and strings pianos have a soundboard. The soundboard makes the vibrations of the strings louder and stronger. Modern pianos have hammers to make the strings vibrate and dampers to quiet them. Foot pedals allow the pianist to damp the strings and control the loudness of the instrument.

Pianos come in two basic shapes. The uprights, which are found in many homes and classrooms, have a rectangular box shape with the keyboard mounted on one side. Grand pianos have a curved triangular shape, with the case of the piano lying horizontally on three stout legs. Grand pianos come in three sizes. The baby grand is a little over 5½ feet long, the drawing room model is 6 to 7 feet long, and the concert grand is from 7 to 9 feet long.

The piano is a very heavy instrument and usually stays in one place, but some concert pianists have their favorite instrument trucked around the country when they go on concert tours. This special effort provides the pianist with a familar instrument and audiences with an opportunity to hear the pianist at his or her best.

HOW TO MAKE AN AEOLIAN HARP
IT'S REALLY A ZITHER

THE AEOLIAN HARP IS A ZITHER THAT IS PLAYED BY THE WIND. YOU PLACE THE INSTRUMENT ON YOUR WINDOW-SILL. YOU NEED A BOARD AS LONG AS YOUR WINDOW IS WIDE, NAILS, STRINGS, AND BRIDGES.

<u>STEP 1</u>. NAIL THE NAILS NEAR THE ENDS OF THE BOARD.

<u>STEP 2</u>. STRETCH MONOFILAMENT OR WIRE STRINGS VERY TIGHT FROM THE NAILS ON ONE END TO THE NAILS ON THE OTHER.

<u>STEP 3</u>. SLIP THE BRIDGES UNDER THE STRINGS INSIDE THE NAILS AT BOTH ENDS. THE BRIDGES HELP STRETCH THE STRINGS AND LIFT THEM SO THEY CAN VIBRATE FREELY.

SET YOUR INSTRUMENT ON THE SILL WITH THE WINDOW OPEN JUST A LITTLE SO THE BREEZE PASSING IN AND OUT IS DIRECTED INTO THE STRINGS. THE MOVING AIR MAKES THE STRINGS VIBRATE. YOU JUST LIE BACK AND LET IT PLAY.

YOU CAN MAKE A LONG, NARROW SOUND BOX THAT WILL FIT YOUR WINDOW. WHEN THE AEOLIAN HARP HAS A SOUND BOX, IT PLAYS EVEN LOUDER.

NAILS

SOUND HOLES

EYE SCREWS

MONOFILAMENT LINE

HOW TO MAKE AN EAR ZITHER

WITH A PIECE OF WOOD ABOUT 6 INCHES SQUARE AND AT LEAST 1/4 INCH THICK, SOME CARPET TACKS, SMALL EYE SCREWS, AND SOME NYLON FISHING LINE YOU CAN MAKE A PRIVATE ZITHER CALLED AN EAR HARP.

TO PLAY THE EAR HARP HOLD THE BACK SIDE OF THE BOARD AGAINST YOUR EAR. STRUM THE STRINGS TO HEAR THE SWEET SOUND. EAR HARPS ARE USUALLY NOT TUNED.

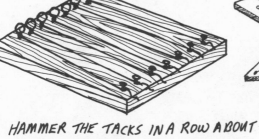

SOME OTHER SHAPES ↓

HAMMER THE TACKS IN A ROW ABOUT 3/8 INCH APART. MAKE A ROW WITH THE EYE SCREWS ALONG THE OPPOSITE EDGE OF THE BOARD. STRETCH THE STRINGS FROM THE TACKS TO THE SCREWS AS TIGHT AS YOU CAN. TIGHTEN THE STRINGS BY TURNING IN THE SCREWS.

Chapter 5
What's an Idiophone?

Wherever you are right now, there are idiophones around you. *Idio* means self and *phone* means sound. Idiophones are self-sounding. The world is full of these instruments, just waiting to be made and played.

If you stomp on the ground or the floor, you are playing an idiophone. When you tap your fork on the table,

you are playing another. As you walk through dry weeds in the late summer and hear seed pods rattle, you are listening to idiophones. Anything that naturally produces a sound when it is hit, shaken, plucked, scraped, rubbed, stomped, or crashed together could be called an idiophone. We're living in a surprisingly musical world!

Shake It, Baby!

When you were a baby, someone handed you a musical instrument to play. You probably played it well and enjoyed it a lot. The instrument was a rattle. Playing rattles is not limited to babies—that's just the beginning. In many kinds of music rattles help provide the rhythm or beat. They are used to accompany singers, dancers, or musicians who are playing other instruments.

Rattles are usually vessels filled with seeds or small stones. When the vessel is shaken, the seeds bang against the sides of the vessel and each other to make sounds. The simplest rattles are made from dried gourds with their own seeds still inside to do the rattling. Vessels are also made of animal skin, clay, wood, tin cans, or plastic bottles. Actually almost anything with a hollow that will let the pellets shake around can be made into a rattle.

Not all rattles have the rattling material inside a vessel. A forked stick and some bottle caps nailed on, vessels with beads strung around the outside, or a cluster of small sticks will also rattle when shaken.

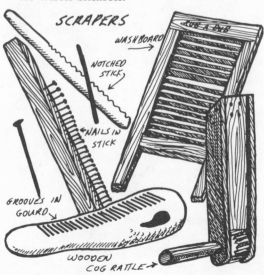

SCRAPERS
WASHBOARD
NOTCHED STICK
NAILS IN STICK
GROOVES IN GOURD
WOODEN COG RATTLE

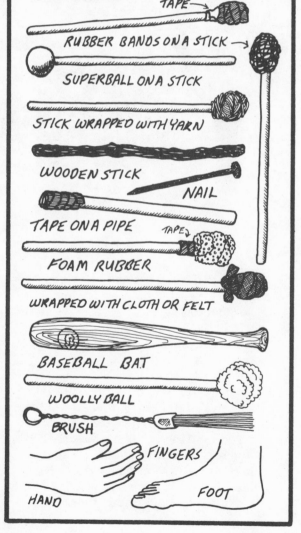

BEATERS
CLICKS FROM THE STICKS

MARIMBAS, BELLS, AND DRUMS ARE SOME OF THE INSTRUMENTS IN THIS BOOK THAT ARE PLAYED WITH BEATERS. BEATERS COME IN ALL SORTS OF SIZES, SHAPES, AND DEGREES OF HARDNESS, AND ARE A KEY PART OF ALL PERCUSSION INSTRUMENTS. FOR SOFT SOUNDS A SOFT BEATER IS USED. FOR CLICKS, DINGS, AND DONGS THE PLAYER TAPS WITH A HARD BEATER. HERE ARE SOME YOU CAN MAKE.

TAPE
RUBBER BANDS ON A STICK
SUPERBALL ON A STICK
STICK WRAPPED WITH YARN
WOODEN STICK
NAIL
TAPE ON A PIPE
TAPE
FOAM RUBBER
WRAPPED WITH CLOTH OR FELT
BASEBALL BAT
WOOLLY BALL
BRUSH
FINGERS
HAND
FOOT

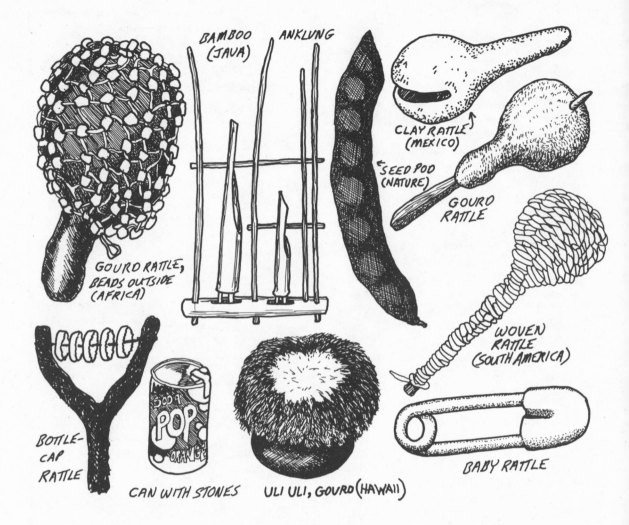

BAMBOO (JAVA) ANKLUNG

CLAY RATTLE (MEXICO)

← SEED POD (NATURE)

GOURD RATTLE

GOURD RATTLE, BEADS OUTSIDE (AFRICA)

WOVEN RATTLE (SOUTH AMERICA)

BOTTLE-CAP RATTLE

BABY RATTLE

CAN WITH STONES   ULI ULI, GOURD (HAWAII)

Jingle All the Way

Like rattles, jingles are shaken to make them sound. Jingles are made of a number of small instruments that wouldn't make a very big sound by themselves, so they are gathered together as a group to make a single, larger, louder instrument.

Jingles are rhythm instruments. They play the beat rather than the melody, or tune. Jingles are especially favored by dancers. Some are shaken as they're held in the dancer's hands. Others are worn on the wrists, legs, ankles, or other parts of the body. As the dancers move and twirl their bodies, these movements cause the jingles to make their sounds.

Jingles are often made of clusters of tiny bells, nuts, seashells, metal disks, little rattles, or pieces of clay strung or hung together. In a certain old Christmas song the horse, of course, wears jingle bells.

You Can Tell It's a Bell

The grandest and most playful sounding of the idiophones are bells. They ring the sounds of celebration and punctuate special moments all over the world. Bells ring out songs of exuberant joy and toll tones of deep sorrow. They awake us from our thoughts to notice danger, someone at the door, cows on the hillside, kittens at play, or breezes passing through the afternoon. Bells remind us that time is passing.

Bells are usually made of metal or wood. They have a deep bowl, or cup, shape. There are thousands of variations of the basic shape. Pellet bells are usually sphere shaped with a slit, or slits, cut to form a line or cross shape. Orchestral chimes, another type of bell, are metal tubes that are suspended from a string tied at one end.

When a bell is struck, it vibrates most near the rim. The area near the vertex vibrates little or not at all.

Bells are struck one of three ways. Pellet bells have an unattached pellet enclosed within the body that bangs against the body when the bell is shaken. Sleigh bells are pellet bells.

Clapper bells have clappers, or beaters, attached either to the inside or outside of the body. The clapper swings into the body of the bell to make it vibrate with a clang. Churchbells and cowbells are clapper bells.

A third type of bell is struck with an unattached beater. Some large bells in temples in Japan are sounded by a suspended log which is swung into them. Smaller bells are struck with beaters like drumsticks to make them sound.

The large metal bells that ring in the towers of churches are usually made of a special alloy (mixture) of metal called bell metal. This mixture of 80 percent copper and 20 percent tin makes an especially rich sound. To cast bells, molten (hot liquid) bell metal is poured into a mold, where it cools to form the bell.

The largest bell in the world is the Czar Kolokol in Moscow, the capital city of the Soviet Union. It weighs 180 tons (that's 360,000 pounds) and is more than 19 feet high. The first time the bell was struck, a 12-ton chunk broke out of it. The broken bell sits on a platform in Kremlin Square for people to view and marvel at.

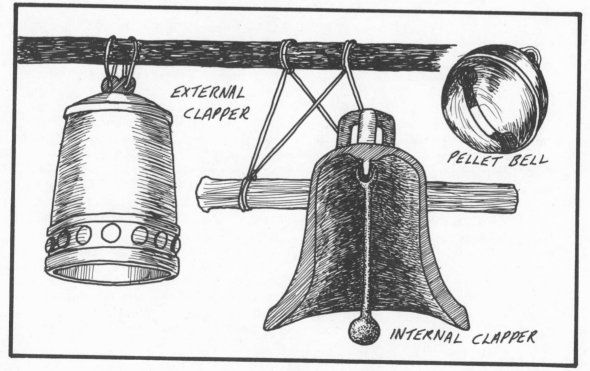

EXTERNAL CLAPPER

PELLET BELL

INTERNAL CLAPPER

59

FLOWERPOT BELLS AND NAIL CHIMES

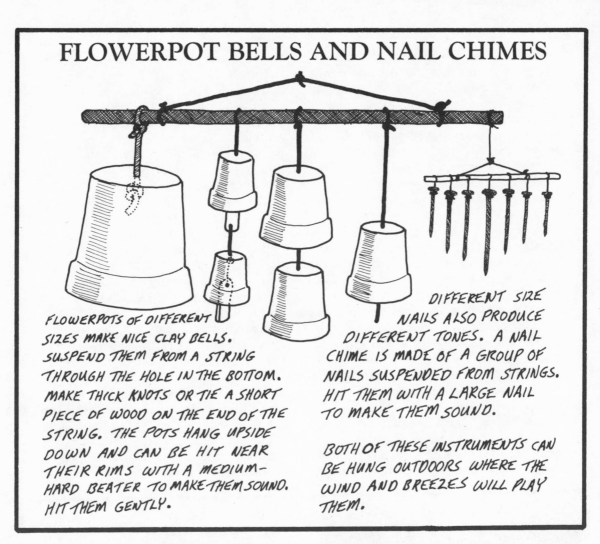

FLOWERPOTS OF DIFFERENT SIZES MAKE NICE CLAY BELLS. SUSPEND THEM FROM A STRING THROUGH THE HOLE IN THE BOTTOM. MAKE THICK KNOTS OR TIE A SHORT PIECE OF WOOD ON THE END OF THE STRING. THE POTS HANG UPSIDE DOWN AND CAN BE HIT NEAR THEIR RIMS WITH A MEDIUM-HARD BEATER TO MAKE THEM SOUND. HIT THEM GENTLY.

DIFFERENT SIZE NAILS ALSO PRODUCE DIFFERENT TONES. A NAIL CHIME IS MADE OF A GROUP OF NAILS SUSPENDED FROM STRINGS. HIT THEM WITH A LARGE NAIL TO MAKE THEM SOUND.

BOTH OF THESE INSTRUMENTS CAN BE HUNG OUTDOORS WHERE THE WIND AND BREEZES WILL PLAY THEM.

In Search of Gongs

Gongs can be made out of any flat piece of metal. When you find a good piece, drill a couple of holes near its rim and tie a length of cord through them for hanging the gong. Hang it so it doesn't touch anything and slam it with a soft beater. Heavier pieces of metal work better than something as thin as a garbage-can lid. Some frying pans make good gongs. Ask your mother first. Bong!

Gong Along

Plagued by demons and evil spirits? Consider a quick trip to Burma to get a Shan drum. This instrument is really a flat gong, set on a drumlike base. It is highly valued for its demon-chasing sound. In Burma the owner of a Shan drum enjoys a social status higher than the owner of seven elephants. Even if you forget the demons and just consider the peanuts it would take to feed seven elephants, this instruments is a bargain.

Gongs are close relatives of bells. Some deep-rimmed gongs are even mistaken for bells, and bells for gongs. The difference is that bells vibrate most near the rim, while gongs vibrate most at the center.

The earliest gongs were flat bronze plates. Now they usually have a bulging surface and/or a raised bump in the center called a "boss."

Gongs are usually suspended from a frame with cords that attach to the edges of the gong. Some, like the Javanese kenong, are played in a horizontal position.

Sometimes sets of tuned gongs are arranged on a frame. The yun lo of China has nine or ten small gongs suspended in rows. The tam-am la-a, once played in Vietnamese court orchestras, is a set of three gongs on one stand. Small gongs often have a bell-like tone; larger ones make sounds from a swishing hiss to a grand bong.

Crash Crop

Cymbals look like gongs and vibrate toward their rims like bells. Because they are sounded in a different way, they belong to neither group. Cymbals come in pairs and are crashed together to make their sound. This type of action is called concussion.

Cymbals are usually made of metal and have a shallow dome or cone shape. They come in a variety of sizes, from finger cymbals, just an inch or two in diameter, to the cymbals played in symphony orchestras, which are sometimes two feet in diameter. The orchestral cymbals make a crash loud enough to awaken sleeping audiences.

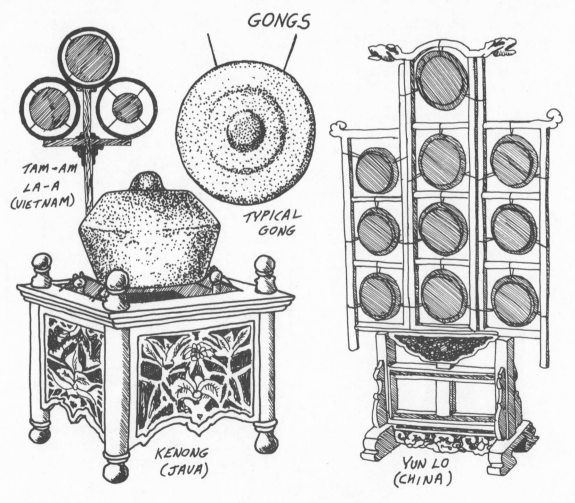

GONGS

TAM-AM LA-A (VIETNAM)

TYPICAL GONG

KENONG (JAVA)

YUN LO (CHINA)

61

There are many other concussion instruments. All make their sound by crashing together two or more similar objects.

The castanets played by flamenco dancers in Spain are small shell-shaped wooden clappers. They hang from the fingers of the player by a string that works like a spring to hold

the two halves apart. The player taps the halves together with her fingers to click them. Very, very rapid rhythms can be played with the castanets.

Not just bodies, but orchestras, too, can contain bones. Musical bones are made from the rib bones of a goat or sheep. To play the bones you dangle them between your fingers as shown below and tap them together with the other fingers to sound their rhythm. Instruments called ''bones'' are sold in music stores, but they are usually made of wood or hard plastic.

THEM BONES

HOLD ONE BONE PRESSED INTO THE PAD BETWEEN THE RING AND MIDDLE FINGER. THIS BONE MUST NEVER TOUCH THE PALM OF THE HAND BECAUSE IT MUST MOVE WHEN YOU FLIP YOUR WRIST. THE BONE HELD BETWEEN THE FIRST AND MIDDLE FINGERS REMAINS STATIONARY. IT SHOULD STICK UP ABOVE THE KNUCKLE ½ INCH HIGHER THAN THE MOVABLE BONE. PRESS THE STATIONARY BONE AGAINST THE HEEL OF THE HAND AND CUP THE HAND AROUND IT. TO GRIP THE BONES PRESS BOTH THE THUMB AND LITTLE FINGER AGAINST THE FINGER NEXT TO THEM. FLIP YOUR WRIST TO CLICK THE BONES TOGETHER.

In your kitchen silverware drawer you can find the raw materials for a clapper called the musical spoons. Hold two spoons parallel with the backs of the scoops facing each other with your index finger between the spoon handles. Then tap them against your

THEM SPOONS

HOLD SPOONS LIKE THIS

1/4"→

BEND HANDLES SO CUPS' BACKS ARE 1/4" APART WHEN THE

SPOONS ARE HELD THIS WAY.

SLAP UP AGAINST YOUR HAND AND DOWN AGAINST YOUR LEG TO PLAY.

other hand or your leg to clink out their friendly sound. It may be awkward at first, but you will get better with practice.

Wood blocks, seashells, fans, cards, stones, coins, sticks, and hands are some of the many things that can be clapped together to make clicking, slapping, and popping sounds.

The sweetest of all clappers is the wind chime. Wood, glass, metal, or clay pieces hang from a frame and strike each other when they are blown by the wind, making a gentle tinkling sound in a breeze.

The No-Cent Stamp

Stamping is another way of making sounds. By far the easiest way is to stamp your feet. Sometimes the thing being stamped makes the sound; sometimes the thing doing the stamping makes most of the music. When you stamp your bare feet on a wooden floor, the floor does most of the vibrating. Dance on cement with wooden-soled or tap-dancing shoes and the shoes do the sounding.

In the Solomon Islands and on the island of New Hebrides bark or boards are used to cover a pit in the ground, so dancers stomp their feet on the boards as they dance. Both the pit and the board or bark cover amplify the sounds of dancing feet and accompany the dancers.

Stamping sticks are also a common and popular instrument. The player hits one end of the stick on the ground to make a sound. Both solid and hollow sticks are used. The hollow ones work especially well, because the column of air inside them resonates with the stick's vibrations. Sticks may be wood, gourd, or bamboo.

In some places people still grind corn and other grains with a mortar and pestle. The mortar is some kind of a bowl, and the pestle is a stick (usually with a thick end). Pounding the stick against the grain and bowl makes a natural rhythm. To the beat of this pounding, people sing songs that make their work easier and more fun.

VIEW OF TOP SHOWING TUNED DENTS →

Stamping Sticks to Steel Drums

On the island of Trinidad in the West Indies every year there is a wild, fun celebration called Carnival. During the two days of Carnival, which is the last big bash before Lent, people wear masks and costumes and go dancing in the streets.

To make music for the dancing, there used to be bamboo tamboo bands composed of hundreds of young people. Each person in the band carried a bamboo stick 3 or 4 inches in diameter and 4 to 6 feet long. When the sticks were pounded on the ground, each making its particular tone, a thundering rhythm-orchestra filled the air with sound.

In 1937 the stick bands were declared illegal. Police said the rival bands were fighting too much and using the sticks to hit each other. With the stamping sticks outlawed people won-

dered how they could make music for Carnival. A search for new musical instruments began. Because many of the people in Trinidad are poor, they could not just run down to the music store and buy new instruments. Instead, they gathered metal cans, pans, automobile parts, and other scraps from junkyards and beat them to make the rhythm-music everyone wanted.

Then somebody discovered that a dent in the bottom of a garbage can made a unique musical note. When hammering out the dent, perhaps, someone noticed the tone changed. Next, experiments with dents of different sizes were made. Each produced a different tone. Within a few years the young people of the island had created, by trial and error, some new musical instruments. Instead of using garbage cans, they hammered dents into the steel oil drums discarded by the petroleum industry on the island.

Steel drums, which are really a type of gong, are now the national instrument of Trinidad. They provide melody and rhythm at Carnival time and all year round on the island. Steel drums are played in bands that may have fifty or more players. Each year at Carnival the band members, their families, and their friends who dance in the streets to their music all celebrate in colorful costumes.

In the 1940s police threatened to ban steel drums, in hopes of taming the Carnival spirit, but this time the whole island protested. So the bands remained to play their music, and today there are several hundred bands on Trinidad.

Playing Junk Music

In the kitchens and junkyards of America and the world, millions of percussion instruments lie waiting to be beaten into sound. Percussion means something is hit to make it sound. Pots, pans, and cans are among the thousands of vessels to be found in the world that can be hit with hands, sticks, or whatever to make sounds. Look around: What "junk" do you have that could be hit to make a sound?

Warning: These instruments and their sounds are not loved equally by everybody. Think of your family's and your neighbors' ears.

Bottles, drinking glasses, cans, and bowls can be tuned for playing melodies by filling sets of them with different amounts of water. The more water you add the lower the pitch will be.

The Indians of the American Southwest play a percussion vessel that is a basket of tightly woven roots and grasses. This bowl-shaped instrument is turned upside down and held against the ground while the player slaps it with her open hands to make a loud drumlike sound.

The Right Way

Have you ever washed dishes and made them squeaky clean? If you have, you've played a friction idiophone. Rubbing produces friction, so objects that sound by rubbing are called friction idiophones. You can make a friction idiophone (it's easier to make it than say it) with a drinking glass.

Find a glass with smooth sides and a smooth rim. A wine glass with a stem, especially one made of thin crystal, usually works quite well. Lots of other kinds of glasses work too.

To play the glass you need to have fingers that are free of grease. That means clean hands. Put a little water in the clean glass, then wet the tip of one of your clean fingers. Rub your finger in a circular motion around the rim of the glass. You may get a tone right away or you may have to rub for a while. Try varying the pressure of your finger and also the speed at which you are rubbing. If you try to play too thick a glass, you may never get it to sound. Try another kind of glass.

The musical glass makes a steady, eerie, high-pitched tone that often sounds like it is coming from somewhere else. If you're not sure it is you making the sound, stop moving your finger. If the sound doesn't stop, check your house for ghosts!

You can change the pitch of your glass by adding or pouring out water. Like the bottles you *tap* on page 65, the more water you put into the glass you *rub,* the lower the pitch will be. It is the glass that is vibrating, not the column of air inside it. Different size glasses will produce different pitches. Try tuning two different size glasses to the same pitch by adding and pouring out water.

WET FINGER FREE OF GREASE

Instruments made of musical glasses are called glass harmonicas. You can make a glass harmonica by gathering several glasses together and tuning them to different pitches. By yourself or with some friends you can figure out and play tunes by rubbing the glasses. At different times in history the glass harmonica has been a popular instrument.

Benjamin Franklin was so fascinated by the glass harmonica and its sweet, eerie sounds that he invented an improved model. Franklin's instrument was called the glass armonica. It had a row of graduated, tuned, glass bowls mounted on a spindle, one inside the other. They were turned by a crank or a treadle over a trough of water that just wetted their rims. By moving his wet finger from one tuned bowl rim to another as the bowls revolved, the player could play a melody.

Glasses and fingers are not the only things that make rubbing music together. The musical saw and the nail violin are rubbed with a violin bow. When wooden blocks covered with sandpaper are rubbed together, they make a ch-ch-ch sound. Bones, stones, pieces of wood, shells, and pinecones are some other materials that can be rubbed to make music. Some rubbing sounds—fingernails rubbing a chalkboard, for example—give some people the creeps!

The Musical Saw

One of the most amazing musical creations on earth is the musical saw. Carpenters make all sorts of sounds as they work, but none have the special appeal and weird, mysterious quality of the musical saw.

The primary piece of equipment for saw players is the saw itself. The kind carpenters use with a flat steel blade about 26 inches long does the trick. You will also need a beater. A thick rubber band wrapped around a stick to make a firm end is good.

Place the handle of the saw between your knees as you sit in a straight-backed chair. The blade sticks up and the teeth face toward your body.

Place your left thumb on the top side of the blade near the end. Hook the fingers of the left hand over the end. Push with the thumb and pull with the fingers to make a bend in the blade. By pushing the left hand toward the floor, make another bend in the blade so it has an "S" curve. It is ready to play.

Tap the blade with the beater. Hit it in different places until it makes a clear "boing" sound. As you push the left hand more toward the floor and hit the saw again, the pitch should rise. As the pitch rises, you will have to hit the blade closer to the end to get a clear tone. To lower the pitch, raise the left arm and hit the blade closer to the handle.

If the saw is not bent in an "S" curve, the only sound you will get when you hit it is the thud of the beater.

To play tunes on the saw, think the melody and bend the blade until the tone matches the tone in your thought. It's helpful to practice with records of songs you like.

Your left thumb will get tired at first but with practice it will get stronger.

When you have a good idea of the places to hit the blade to produce clear sounds, you are ready to graduate to using a bow. A violin bow is preferred, but you can also make one by stretching a thick cotton string across a wooden bow. The string needs to be rosined to make the saw vibrate.

You bow the saw on the back, the smooth side. If you bow the side with the teeth, you will soon rip your bow to shreds. Bow with short strokes perpendicular to the blade. Move the bow up and down the blade each time you change the pitch.

Give the musical saw a try. At worst you'll have a creepy noisemaker in time for Halloween.

Just Scraping By

By cutting a row of notches in a stick and rubbing over them with a nail or stick, you can make and play a scraped idiophone (a scraper, for short). These instruments make a zipperlike sound. In fact, a zipper is a scraped idiophone. Scrapers have been around since the Stone Age. Some scrapers are made of bones, stones, or notched gourds, but mostly they are made of wood.

You can make a nail scraper by nailing a row of nails along a board and scraping them with another nail. You can run a stick along a picket fence to make it sound, or your thumbnail across a comb.

Washboards were invented for washing clothes, but they soon found their way into the instrument world, especially in jug bands. A metal rod or thimbles on the player's fingers scraped across the corrugated surface of the washboard makes a razzmatazz rattle.

Another way of getting the scraped sound is with a ratchet. Ratchets, or cog rattles, have a notched wheel that rubs against a tongue of wood or metal and makes a click-click sound. By clothespinning some playing cards on the fork of your bicycle so the spokes flip the cards when the wheel turns, you can make a traveling ratchet. This instrument makes your bike sound a little like a motorcycle and announces to everybody that you're scraping by.

Here's Loads About Nodes

It seems to make sense that when you hit an object, the entire object vibrates. But one of the amazing things about a vibrating chunk of matter is that it does not all vibrate at once. You can check this out with a couple of simple experiments.

Node Patterns

Ernst Chladni, who lived from 1756 to 1827, discovered the method of sprinkling sand on solids to find nodal points. He experimented by sprinkling sand on steel disks and watched the patterns change as he played various notes on a violin. As the pitch of the sound changed, the patterns of the sand also changed. The organic and geometrical patterns the sand formed included concentric rings, six-sided honeycombs,

THE DUST TEST

THIS TEST ISN'T FOR SEEING HOW CLEAN YOUR CLOTHES ARE. IT IS A GOOD WAY TO FIND NODES ON A FLAT VIBRATING SOLID OBJECT. GET A PIECE OF WOOD ABOUT 3/4 INCH THICK, 1 OR 2 INCHES WIDE, AND 1 FOOT LONG. SET THE WOOD ON TWO STRIPS OF FOAM RUBBER, FELT, OR TWO STRETCHED STRINGS. SET IT ON SOMETHING SO IT CAN VIBRATE FREELY.

SPRINKLE SAND, SALT, SAWDUST, OR DIRT ON THE TOP SURFACE OF THE BAR.

TAP THE BAR WITH A BEATER — A STICK OR KNUCKLE WILL DO THE JOB. TAP FIRMLY, BUT NOT BRUTALLY. IT DOESN'T MATTER WHERE YOU HIT IT. CONTINUE TAPPING OFTEN ENOUGH TO KEEP THE BAR VIBRATING. WHAT HAPPENS TO THE PARTICLES? TRY AGAIN WITH THE FOAM STRIPS IN DIFFERENT PLACES.

THE LISTENING TEST

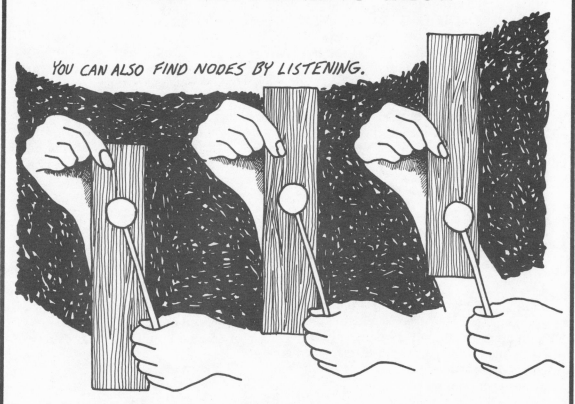

YOU CAN ALSO FIND NODES BY LISTENING.

WITH YOUR THUMB AND FOREFINGER HOLD THE BOARD NEAR ONE END. AS YOU DANGLE IT NEAR YOUR EAR, TAP THE BOARD WITH A BEATER. LISTEN TO THE SOUND IT MAKES.

NEXT HOLD THE BOARD AT A POINT ABOUT ONE-FOURTH OF ITS LENGTH FROM ONE OF THE ENDS. TAP AND LISTEN.

HOLD IT IN THE MIDDLE. TAP AND LISTEN.

FIND THE SPOT WHERE YOU CAN HOLD IT AND IT MAKES THE LOUDEST, LONGEST-LASTING SOUND. YOU WILL HAVE FOUND A NODE.

THERE ARE TWO NODES ON A _FREELY VIBRATING_ BAR OF WOOD, METAL, OR ANY OTHER SOLID MATERIAL. THEY ARE LOCATED ABOUT ONE-FOURTH OF THE LENGTH FROM THE ENDS. TEST DIFFERENT LENGTHS AND MATERIALS TO FIND THE NODES. "FREELY VIBRATING" MEANS THE BOARD IS HELD LOOSELY AND ALLOWED TO VIBRATE IN ITS NATURAL STATE WITHOUT ANY APPLIED TENSION.

IF YOU CLAMP A BOARD SECURELY, THE POSITION OF THE NODES WILL MOVE.

spirals, pentagonal stars, and other patterns that occur in nature.

Chladni's method later allowed Felix Savart to explore the nodal patterns of the violin. He made violin-shaped plates and watched which places vibrated when certain notes were played. He hoped to learn ways to make violins sound better.

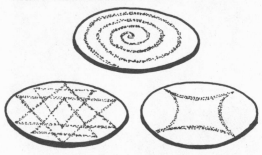

Hans Jenny of Zurich spent ten years duplicating and expanding Chladni's experiments. He used sophisticated equipment and filmed his experiments. He named this study cymatics, the study of the interrelationship of wave forms with matter.

The Marimba

The marimba is an instrument that makes use of freely vibrating bars or platens of wood. It is a xylophone (xylo means wood). Some marimbas are very simple. Others are made from special woods, are carefully tuned, and have elaborate decorations. In North America they are often children's toys, but in South America and Africa the marimbas are used just for play on special occasions. They are called different names in different places, but they all work just about the same way.

The bars of wood are arranged parallel to each other. They usually rest on strips of a soft material or are tied together through holes drilled in, or grooves cut around, them at their nodes. The bars make their best sounds if they do not touch each other or any

other solid material that would keep them from vibrating freely. To produce sound the player hits the bars with a beater.

One of the things that makes marimbas possible is the fact that every piece of wood in the world, from gigantic logs to tiny twigs, has a free vibration of its own. When a piece of wood is hit and allowed to vibrate freely, it will always vibrate the same number of times per second. Some pieces may vibrate too slowly or without enough strength to allow you to hear them. Some pieces are too large or too small to make into reasonable instruments. There are billions of chunks of wood with sizes, shapes, and sounds that make them ideal for instruments. You can find wood for your marimba experiments in alleys, dumpsters, or near construction sites, and, of course, in parks and forests.

**You Wood Be
Tuning In**

The marimbas you have constructed so far make whatever tones the pieces of wood naturally make. They probably don't sound like the marimbas you could buy in a music store. Those instruments are tuned. Musicians usually need instruments tuned to make very particular sounds because that makes it possible for them to play along with other instruments. A great many of the musical instruments

HOW TO MAKE MARIMBAS

YOU CAN MAKE A BASIC MARIMBA BY PLACING TWO OR THREE BOARDS ACROSS YOUR OUTSTRETCHED LEGS.

YOU'VE PROBABLY ALREADY FIGURED OUT THE LEG AND WOOD MARIMBA IS NOT QUITE AS COMMON AS THE TYPE IN WHICH THE BARS ARE ATTACHED TO A FRAME. THE BARS ARE USUALLY PLACED ALONG STRIPS OF FELT OR FOAM RUBBER OR SUSPENDED ON CORDS LIKE A SUSPENSION BRIDGE.

REST THE BOARDS ON YOUR LEGS AT THE NODES SO THEY CAN VIBRATE FREELY. USE A STICK, STONE, OR YOUR FIST FOR A BEATER AND YOU ARE IN THE MUSIC GAME. THE LONGER YOUR LEGS AND ARMS, THE MORE BOARDS YOU CAN ADD—A MUSICAL INSTRUMENT THAT GROWS WITH YOU!

TO MAKE ONE, GATHER A COLLECTION OF STICKS THAT SOUND PLEASANT TO YOU. THEN EITHER DRILL HOLES IN THEM OR CARVE OR FILE GROOVES AROUND THEM AT THE NODES. MAKE OR FIND A FRAME (A BOX WORKS) AND SET UP YOUR MARIMBA.

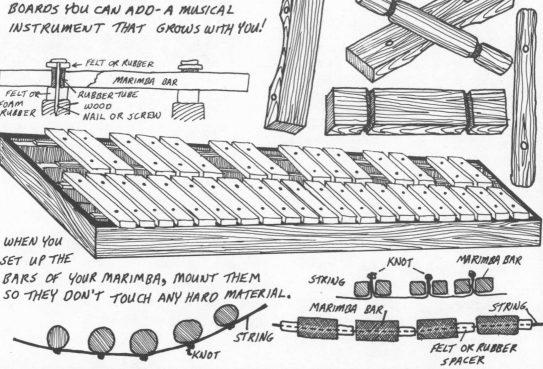

WHEN YOU SET UP THE BARS OF YOUR MARIMBA, MOUNT THEM SO THEY DON'T TOUCH ANY HARD MATERIAL.

manufactured in the world today are tuned to play standard pitches. This saves musicians a lot of confusion.

You're a marimba maker! You, too, can change and control the sound a bar of wood will make. It is often at this point in instrument making that people panic. Hands are thrown up in despair. People gasp and make statements like: "I could never do that" and "I am tone deaf." "I just don't have any talent," some say timidly. If you *must* panic, do it now. Clear out your system. Take a deep breath and read on.

Imagine you have a bar of wood. Bet-

ter yet, get one. You hit it and it makes a particular sound. You had another sound in mind. This one just won't do. Now the fun begins. You can either raise or lower the pitch. Both operations are simple.

Practice a little to get the feel of it. Try matching the pitch of two pieces of wood that are different lengths. If you are going to make a shorter piece sound like a longer one, you will *usually* need to lower its pitch. To make the longer one sound like a shorter one, you will *usually* have to raise its pitch.

TUNE UP

TO <u>LOWER</u> THE PITCH OF A BAR, SAW OR CARVE A SLIT ACROSS THE MIDDLE OF THE BOTTOM SIDE.

THE DEEPER YOU CUT THE SLIT, THE LOWER THE PITCH BECOMES.

IF THE PITCH NEEDS TO BE <u>LOWERED</u> A LOT, USE A WOOD CHISEL AND/OR A WOOD RASP TO CARVE A GENTLE

ARCH ON THE BOTTOM OF THE BAR. IF YOU FILE OR CARVE TOO DEEPLY, YOU CAN <u>RAISE</u> THE PITCH BY SAWING OR FILING A LITTLE WOOD OFF THE ENDS.

FILE SOME OFF — OR SAW OFF A PIECE. THE PITCH RISES.

TUNING A PIECE OF WOOD IS MAGICAL. YOU REALLY OUGHT TO TRY. YOU WILL BE AMAZED!

TRY MAKING TWO DIFFERENT SIZE PIECES SOUND THE SAME.

TONE DEAF ??

A VERY SMALL NUMBER OF PEOPLE - ONE OUT OF A HUNDRED THOUSAND OR MORE - ARE ACTUALLY TONE DEAF. EVEN IF SOMEONE HAS TOLD YOU THAT YOU ARE TONE DEAF, CHANCES ARE THAT YOU ARE ABLE TO HEAR DIFFERENT TONES. WITH A LITTLE PRACTICE YOU PROBABLY WILL GET BETTER AT HEARING TONES. TUNING PIECES OF WOOD OR GLASSES OF WATER, PAGE 65, ARE GOOD WAYS TO PRACTICE. GET HELP FROM A FRIEND WHO HEARS TONES EASILY AND USE YOUR VOICES TO PRACTICE MATCHING TONES.

Notice that word "usually." The length is not the only factor affecting how fast or slow a piece of wood will vibrate. Because every piece of wood forms (grows) under different conditions (soil, moisture, sunlight, wind), each is unique and different. If you had two pieces exactly the same size but one was softer than the other, it would have a lower pitch. If two pieces were the same length and width but one was thicker than the other, it would have a higher pitch.

Resonators

A column of air is a chunk of matter, so it has a lot in common with a piece of wood. It has different characteristics, too, but it is a chunk of matter all the same. Each column of free air ("free air" means it is not under pressure or completely enclosed) has a natural pitch just like each piece of wood, metal, or any other substance does. The longer the column of air is, the lower its natural pitch is, the shorter, the higher.

You can make a column of free air by holding a can with one end open or a water glass right side up. The air inside is a free column of air the length of the container. It's that simple.

When a column of free air has exactly the same natural pitch as a bar on your marimba, they are in resonance. When the bar vibrates, it makes all the air in the column vibrate, and the sound becomes much louder. If the air and the bar have different natural pitches, the column of air won't help the bar sound louder.

By making columns of free air of various lengths, you can make resonators for your marimba, and it will sound much louder when you play it.

Metal and Stone on the Phone

Wood is not the only kind of material that can make sound when it is hit. You probably make a sound when you're hit! But some of these musical materials can also be tuned.

When marimbalike instruments are made of metal they are called metallophones. The wonderful orchestras on the islands of Bali and Java include metallophones. The glockenspiel and the celesta are members of this group that are played in the symphony orchestra.

The celesta looks like a upright piano, but instead of having strings inside, it has metal bars. The bars are hit by hammers to make them sound. The player pushes a key, like a piano key, to make the hammer strike the bar. Each bar has its own resonator to make the sound louder.

The glockenspiel looks like a marimba with metal bars. The glockenspiel's bars are usually set up in two rows in a carrying case. The name *glockenspiel* in German means "bell-play." The name suits the instrument, which has a bright, ringing tone.

In the same way you can tune wooden bars you can also tune bars and tubes of metal. With pieces of metal the same height, weight, and density, a longer piece will have a lower pitch than a shorter piece when it is struck.

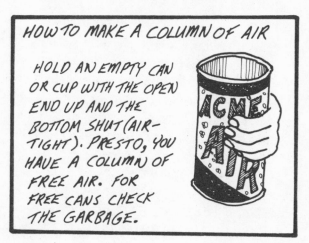

HOW TO MAKE A COLUMN OF AIR

HOLD AN EMPTY CAN OR CUP WITH THE OPEN END UP AND THE BOTTOM SHUT (AIR-TIGHT). PRESTO, YOU HAVE A COLUMN OF FREE AIR. FOR FREE CANS CHECK THE GARBAGE.

HOW TO MAKE
MAGICAL MARIMBA RESONATORS

TO MAKE COLUMNS OF FREE AIR THAT WILL RESONATE WITH YOUR MARIMBA'S BARS YOU NEED TUBES WITH SEALED BOTTOMS. THE MATERIAL THE TUBE IS MADE OF SHOULD BE AS THIN AND HARD AS YOU CAN FIND. TIN CANS TAPED TOGETHER OR SAWED OFF MAKE SUPER RESONATORS, AND THEY ARE EASY TO FIND. <u>BE CAREFUL OF SHARP OR JAGGED METAL EDGES.</u>

FIRST MAKE A TEST RESONATOR. SELECT CANS THAT HAVE A DIAMETER A LITTLE WIDER THAN THE WIDTH OF THE MARIMBA BARS. CUT THE TOPS AND BOTTOMS OUT OF A COUPLE OF THE CANS. WITH BLACK PLASTIC ELECTRICAL TAPE OR MASKING TAPE JOIN THE CANS TO MAKE ONE TALL CAN. TAPE THE JOINTS <u>TIGHT</u> SO WATER WON'T LEAK OUT.

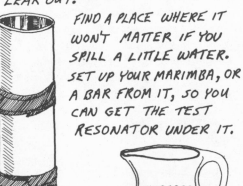

FIND A PLACE WHERE IT WON'T MATTER IF YOU SPILL A LITTLE WATER. SET UP YOUR MARIMBA, OR A BAR FROM IT, SO YOU CAN GET THE TEST RESONATOR UNDER IT.

BOTTOM ON THIS CAN

BOOKS FOR WEIGHT

HOLD THE CAN SO ITS OPENING IS AN INCH OR LESS BELOW THE BAR. TAP THE BAR AND LISTEN. DOES THE CAN MAKE THE BAR SOUND LOUDER? ☐ A LITTLE ☐ A LOT ☐ NOT AT ALL ADD A LITTLE (ABOUT ½-INCH) WATER, TAP AND LISTEN, ADD SOME MORE AND CONTINUE TO TAP THE BAR. YOU ARE LISTENING FOR THE SOUND TO BECOME LOUDER, FOR THE COLUMN OF AIR INSIDE THE CAN TO COME INTO RESONANCE WITH THE BAR. WHEN IT HAPPENS, YOU WILL KNOW. IF YOU AREN'T SURE, CONTINUE TO FILL THE CAN AND TAP THE BAR.

IF THE SOUND GETS LOUDER, THEN WHEN YOU ADD A LITTLE MORE WATER IT GETS SOFTER, YOU WILL KNOW YOU HAVE FILLED THE CAN PAST THE POINT OF RESONANCE. POUR OUT A LITTLE WATER AND TRY AGAIN FOR THE LOUDEST POSSIBLE SOUND. IF YOU FILL THE CAN ALL THE WAY TO THE TOP AND THE BAR DIDN'T SOUND LOUDER (THIS WILL PROBABLY HAPPEN ONLY IF YOU HAVE A VERY LARGE BAR), POUR

(CONTINUED) →

RESONATORS
(CONTINUED)

OUT ALL THE WATER AND TAPE ANOTHER CAN (WITHOUT A BOTTOM) TO THE TOP OF THE RESONATOR. THEN START FILLING THE LONGER COLUMN UNTIL IT COMES INTO RESONANCE. REMEMBER, THE HIGHER THE PITCH, THE SHORTER THE COLUMN OF AIR INSIDE THE CANS WILL BE.

WHEN YOU HAVE FOUND THE WATER LEVEL WHERE THE SOUND IS LOUDEST, MEASURE FROM THE TOP OF THE CAN TO THE TOP OF THE WATER.

THIS IS THE LENGTH YOUR RESONATOR NEEDS TO BE IF YOU USE CANS THAT HAVE THE SAME DIAMETER AS YOUR TEST CAN. TO SHORTEN CANS A HACKSAW WORKS BEST.

STEPS

VISE

IT HELPS TO BRACE YOUR CAN WHILE YOU SAW. PERHAPS A VISE, A BENCH, STEPS, OR A FRIEND COULD HELP HOLD IT. WHEN CUTTING THIN METAL LIKE A TIN CAN, THE SAW SOMETIMES SNAGS. A SNAGGED SAW CAN BE FRUSTRATING. TO GET THE JOB DONE YOU NEED TO RELAX. EASE UP ON THE SAW, TAKE A DEEP BREATH, SMILE, AND START SAWING AGAIN- GENTLY.

WHEN YOUR RESONATOR IS SAWED TO THE LENGTH YOU WANT, CAP THE ROUGH (SHARP!) EDGE WITH MASKING TAPE. WRAP THE TAPE

AROUND THE EDGE, THEN FOLD IT OVER TO COVER THE ROUGH EDGE.

COVERING THE EDGE DOESN'T AFFECT THE SOUND. IT DOES PROTECT YOU AND YOUR FRIENDS FROM GETTING CUT.

ATTACH THE RESONATORS SO THEY HANG ABOUT AN INCH BELOW THE BARS THEY ARE MADE TO RESONATE WITH.

YOU CAN POKE HOLES IN THEM NEAR THE TOP AND STRING THE CANS LIKE BEADS. TIE A KNOT BEFORE AND AFTER EACH CAN TO SPACE THEM JUST BELOW THE BARS THEY BELONG WITH. YOU CAN ALSO NAIL, SCREW, OR TIE THEM ALONG A BOARD. NAIL THAT BOARD TO THE MARIMBA FRAME.

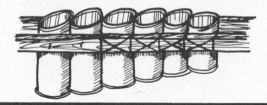

The nodes on a metal bar are located in the same places as those on wooden ones: about one-fourth the length of the bar from the ends.

Do you think stones can be tuned to make musical instruments? The Chinese make an instrument called pien ch'ing from stone. It has L-shaped stones that hang on strings in rows from a frame. The stones are all cut to the same size and shape. To give them different pitches they are carved and ground to different thicknesses.

West Africans play an instrument

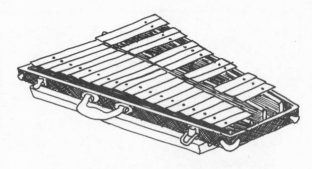

made of several large flat stones. The musician hits the larger stones, as they lie on the ground, with small stones held in his hands. No, this is not how rock and roll got started!

A TUBULAR GLOCKENSPIEL
IT'S AS FUN TO PLAY AS IT IS TO SAY

THE TUBULAR GLOCKENSPIEL HAS A BRILLIANT RINGING TONE. IT IS MADE FROM ELECTRICAL CONDUIT (PIPE). THE ONE WE'LL MAKE USES 1/2-INCH DIAMETER CONDUIT. YOU CAN BUY A 10-FOOT PIECE OF CONDUIT IN A HARDWARE STORE FOR A COUPLE OF DOLLARS. YOU CAN MAKE GLOCKENSPIELS FROM OTHER SIZES OF CONDUIT OR METAL PIPE, TOO, BUT YOU WILL HAVE TO TUNE THEM BY EAR.

WITH A HACKSAW CUT YOUR TUBE TO THESE EXACT LENGTHS: 11", 10 1/4", 9 3/4", 9 1/2", 8 7/8", 8 1/2", 7 7/8", AND 7 5/8".

NOW YOU HAVE A SET OF TUBES ALREADY TUNED TO A MAJOR SCALE.
SET THE TUBES ON TWO STRIPS OF

FOAM RUBBER OR FELT. PLACE THE STRIPS UNDER THE NODES TO ALLOW THE TUBES TO VIBRATE FREELY.

YOU CAN MAKE A GOOD BEATER BY WRAPPING THE END OF A SCRAP OF YOUR CONDUIT WITH THREE OR FOUR LAYERS OF TAPE. MAKE ADDITIONAL TUBES IF YOU LIKE. REMEMBER THE SHORTER THE TUBE, THE HIGHER ITS PITCH WILL BE.

The Gamelan

The people of Bali and Java, two neighboring islands in Indonesia, make music with a special orchestra called the gamelan. Legends tell how the gamelans were played even before there were people on the islands.

On Java, Sang Hjang Batara Guru, king of the gods, made a giant gong. He used it to signal to the lesser gods on the island. But he had more to say than he could clearly communicate with just one gong. His signals confused the lesser gods, who couldn't understand what he had on his mind. To solve the problem he made a second gong that was tuned to a different pitch. Then when he sent signals that were made up of patterns of pitches, things were better, and when the musical language outgrew these two gongs, a third one was made. He called the set of three "gamelan Munggang." Time passed.

Hundreds of years later people came to Java. The old king of the gods was reborn as the god-king Sri Panduka Maharadja Dewabudda. He remembered the three gongs from his previous life and created a place where sacred singing and dancing could be accompanied by the three gongs of the gamelan Munggang. As the years passed, the people made other instruments and formed gamelan orchestras. The instruments of the gamelan orchestra are treated with great respect because they are said to have humanlike spirits. The music they make provides a magical bridge between the people and their gods.

Gamelan orchestras play an important part in the lives of their villages. Although they vary in size and kinds of instruments, a typical orchestra might include a:

Kenong, a large bowl-shaped gong resting in cords on a decorated wood stand.

Gong ageng, two suspended gongs, one about 2 feet across and the other about 3 feet.

Bonnang, a set of tuned, wide-rimmed gongs resting in two rows on cords in a wooden frame.

Gambang kayu, a peacock-shaped xylophone.

Saron demong, a metallophone with a dragon-shaped body.

Ganza gambang and a *ganza jonkok,* metallophones with cradle-shaped bow resonators.

Chengcheng and *rinchik,* cymbals mounted on stands and hit from above with cymbals held in the player's hands.

Two-headed, cylinder-shaped drum and a *spike fiddle.*

Gamelan of Voices

Look at the names of the instruments in the Javanese gamelan orchestra. Say them. The names are an old friend of ours: *onomatopoeia,* words that sound like what they describe. You can make your own gamelan orchestra just by using these names.

Gather a group of your friends. Assign each person the name of a gamelan instrument. Have them say the word over several times to get used to it. Look at the pictures of the instruments in this book and imagine how they might be played. Say the words fast, slow, high, low, lots of different ways.

After everyone has practiced, one person begins by sing-saying his or her word and setting up a rhythm. Perhaps a regular, slow repetition of the name "kenong" will be a good one to start. Then another singer joins in with a different name repeated at a different speed. Then another, and another, and another until all the names are being sing-said. This "game-o-lon" works best if everyone listens and works together. See just how beautiful and interesting a sound your orchestra will make. Don't worry about doing it right —just think about making the sounds work together.

In Java and Bali individual gamelan orchestras have names that tell about the character of their sound. One might be named "gentle wind," another "water running over stones." Make up a name that expresses the character of your gamelan of voices.

Hold Your Tongue

The fact that a flexible tongue of wood or metal can vibrate and create sounds makes Jew's harps and thumb pianos possible.

The Jew's harp has a single wooden or metal tongue attached to a small frame. The tongue is free at one end so it can vibrate when it is plucked. The player holds the frame inside his mouth and plucks the tongue with his thumb. The cavity of the mouth acts as a resonator for the quiet vibrations made by the tongue. In order to make a loud sound the player must shape his mouth to just the right shape so that the air in it will be in resonance with the pitch of the vibrating tongue. The idea is simple enough, but it takes practice to play a twanging Jew's harp well.

Jew's harps are found mostly in Europe, North America, and the islands of Oceania. How they got their name nobody knows for sure, but it is certain they are not Jewish in origin.

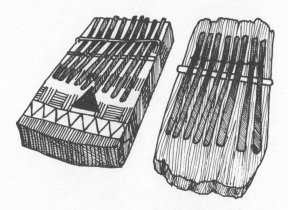

Thumb pianos come from Africa where they have names like sansa, mbira, and kalimba. Their gentle sound is made by plucking the wooden, bamboo, or metal tongues. The tongues are mounted in or on a resonator gourd or box. They are tuned by sliding them forward or backward in their mounting. As the length of the vibrating part of the tongue is changed, naturally the pitch changes. To play a thumb piano the player holds the box or gourd in her hands and plucks the tongues with her thumbs.

Forest of Drums

Related to the marimba and thumb piano are some wonderful drums. These idiophones are made of wood and are usually something like a hollowed tree.

Slit drums are the most common wooden drums and come from many parts of the world. The largest are found in Africa and in the islands of the South Pacific.

In India near the Burmese border, the Naga people make logs into carved and decorated drums that have their

HOW TO MAKE A THUMB PIANO

YOU NEED POPSICLE STICKS, A A CHUNK OF WOOD ABOUT 6 x 6 INCHES SQUARE AND 3/4 INCH THICK, WOOD SCREWS, A DRILL, SCREWDRIVER, AND SOME SMALL STICKS TO MAKE A THUMB PIANO.

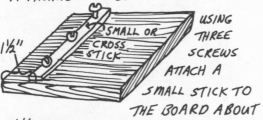

USING THREE SCREWS ATTACH A SMALL STICK TO THE BOARD ABOUT 1½ INCHES FROM ONE SIDE. OR YOU CAN DRILL HOLES THROUGH THE BOARD AND LACE THE SMALL STICK TO IT WITH STRONG STRING, LEATHER, OR WIRE IF YOU WANT. ARRANGE

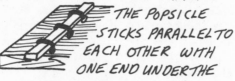

THE POPSICLE STICKS PARALLEL TO EACH OTHER WITH ONE END UNDER THE CROSS STICK.

TIGHTEN THE SCREWS SO THE CROSS STICK <u>ALMOST</u> TOUCHES THE POPSICLE STICKS. SLIP A THIN STICK UNDER THE POPSICLE STICKS AT THEIR LONG ENDS.

A ¼-INCH DOWEL OR TWO OR THREE POPSICLE STICKS STACKED ON EACH OTHER WILL WORK FOR THIS JOB.

PUSH THE STICK AS FAR TOWARD THE CROSS STICK AS IT WILL GO

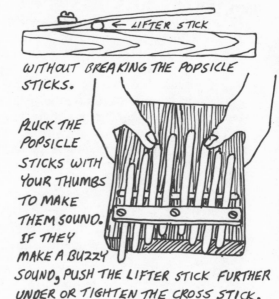

WITHOUT BREAKING THE POPSICLE STICKS.

PLUCK THE POPSICLE STICKS WITH YOUR THUMBS TO MAKE THEM SOUND. IF THEY MAKE A BUZZY SOUND, PUSH THE LIFTER STICK FURTHER UNDER OR TIGHTEN THE CROSS STICK.

TUNE YOUR THUMB PIANO BY PUSHING IN THE POPSICLE STICKS OR PULLING THEM OUT. THE LONGER THE VIBRATING PART, THE LOWER THE PITCH. BECAUSE EVERY PIECE OF WOOD IS DIFFERENT, YOU HAVE TO TUNE YOUR THUMB PIANO BY EAR. YOU CAN MAKE A LOUDER THUMB PIANO BY ATTACHING THE POPSICLE STICKS TO A SMALL SOUND BOX. MAKE IT ABOUT 6 x 6 x 1½ INCHES.

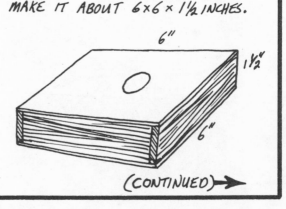

(CONTINUED)→

THUMB PIANO
(CONTINUED)

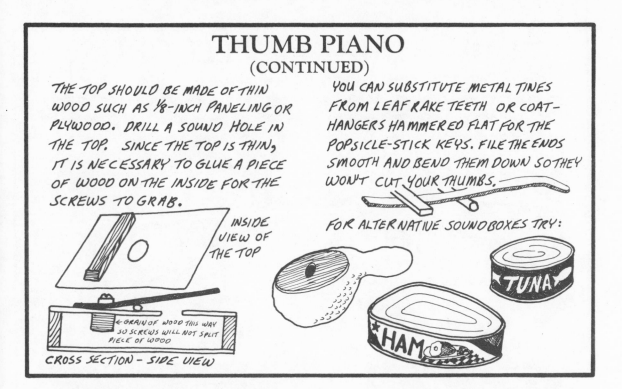

THE TOP SHOULD BE MADE OF THIN WOOD SUCH AS ⅛-INCH PANELING OR PLYWOOD. DRILL A SOUND HOLE IN THE TOP. SINCE THE TOP IS THIN, IT IS NECESSARY TO GLUE A PIECE OF WOOD ON THE INSIDE FOR THE SCREWS TO GRAB.

INSIDE VIEW OF THE TOP

← GRAIN OF WOOD THIS WAY SO SCREWS WILL NOT SPLIT PIECE OF WOOD

CROSS SECTION - SIDE VIEW

YOU CAN SUBSTITUTE METAL TINES FROM LEAF RAKE TEETH OR COAT-HANGERS HAMMERED FLAT FOR THE POPSICLE-STICK KEYS. FILE THE ENDS SMOOTH AND BEND THEM DOWN SO THEY WON'T CUT YOUR THUMBS.

FOR ALTERNATIVE SOUNDBOXES TRY:

TUNA

HAM

own houses. These 30- to 40-foot-long instruments lie on a stand and have roofs built over them to protect them from rain.

On the islands of New Hebrides tree drums are made by hollowing out logs and standing them upright. These drums sometimes stand more than 18 feet tall. They are hollowed out so there is only a thin shell of wood their entire length. Only top and bottom remain solid. A long narrow slit about 4 inches wide runs from near the bottom to up to two-thirds the length. Just above and below the slit are round holes about the same width as the slit is wide. The people who make these drums decorate them with carvings of faces and geometric designs. Some look like totem poles.

To play these drums, which are often set up in groups that look like forests of tall tree stumps, the players hit them with clubs. Of course, the tones of different size drums are different. By hitting different logs, and the same log

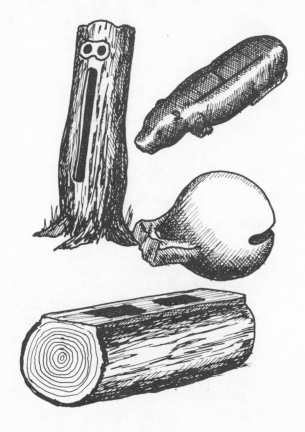

HOW TO MAKE A SLIT DRUM

TO MAKE A SLIT DRUM YOU NEED A COPING SAW, DRILL, GLUE, AND WOOD. THE PIECE OF WOOD FOR THE TOP NEEDS TO BE 4 OR 5 INCHES WIDE, 10 TO 12 INCHES LONG, AND ABOUT 3/4 INCH THICK. IT MUST BE FREE OF KNOTS.*

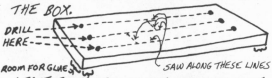

THIS TOP WILL BE GLUED TO A BOX. MAKE A SOUND BOX (PAGE 32) WITH A THIN BOTTOM, 1/8 OR 1/4 INCH IF POSSIBLE.

DESIGN THE TOP SO IT HAS 4 OR 5 "TONGUES." BECAUSE YOU CAN SAW CURVES AND TURN CORNERS WITH A COPING SAW, THE TONGUES CAN BE ANY LONG SHAPE, BUT THEY MUST ATTACH AT ONE END AND BE FREE TO VIBRATE NEAR THE MIDDLE OF THE BOX.

DRILL HERE

ROOM FOR GLUE

SAW ALONG THESE LINES

LEAVE ROOM AROUND THE EDGES TO GLUE THE TOP TO THE SIDES OF YOUR BOX. DRILL 1/4-INCH HOLES IN THE TOP AT THE ENDS OF LINES SO YOU CAN TURN THE SAW BLADE WITHOUT REMOVING IT. PUT THE COPING SAW BLADE THROUGH ONE OF YOUR HOLES. TIGHTEN THE BLADE, THEN SAW ALONG YOUR DESIGN TO MAKE THE TONGUES.

IT HELPS IF YOU CLAMP YOUR BOARD TO THE TABLE OR HOLD IT SO THE SAW IS WORKING NEAR THE EDGE OF THE TABLE. WHEN THE TONGUES HAVE BEEN SAWED, GLUE THE TOP TO THE BOX. WHEN THE GLUE IS DRY, BEAT THE TONGUES WITH RUBBER-ENDED OR SUPERBALL BEATERS AND START TALKING DRUM!

*KNOTS IN WOOD LOOK LIKE THIS.

in different places, the player can produce many tones.

Most slit drums of the world are played in the horizontal position (lying down).

Slit drums are commonly used to send messages. When they are played by a skilled drummer, they can be heard miles away. The messages are sent in drum language, a code of tones and beats that can be understood by the natives. Talking drums allow the people who use them to send detailed messages quickly across distances and through dense jungles. One drummer starts the signal and others deeper in the jungle repeat it so the next group of people can hear. They pass it on to the next and so on. Soon everybody who understands the drum code knows the news.

The slit drums of Africa, India, and Mexico are often carved in the shape of animals. A Japanese slit drum called the mokugyo is carved to look like a ferocious fish.

Chapter 6

Slappin' Skins

The most common form of drum has a stretched skin or thin membrane of some sort. Just as you've been doing, people use what they have or can find around them to make their music makers. In Africa zebra skin or the skins of large snakes are often used. Deerskins are stretched over the ends of hollowed chunks of logs in wooded countries. Eskimos stretch the bladders of seals over wooden hoops and then beat the rhythms of the Arctic. Drummers in rock bands pound furiously on skins of Mylar, a kind of plastic. Drums with a skin belong to a family called membranophones. The sound is produced by the vibrating membrane.

Drums of some sort are used by every culture on earth. The fact certainly suggests that it's human nature to pound out a beat. In many simple societies the drums are treated with great respect and are highly valued for spiritual purposes. In cultures with more advanced technologies the instruments may be respected less, but they still provide the heartbeat that helps connect the music of life to people.

The da-diako is a gigantic drum suspended in a carved and painted frame. It is played in religious ceremonies in Japan. The tom-toms of American Indians provide the beat and soul for their religious dances and ceremonies. Drums are universal noble instruments, simple and rich. The sound can be loud and boisterous, strange and scary, or quiet and sad.

Aside from their spiritual functions, drums serve people in work, play, and communications. You know that signals are sent by drums. Thumping drums have excited and encouraged soldiers as they marched to battle. Drummers set the pace for groups working together (such as people picking crops or swinging hammers). They build up excitement at games, parades, and festivals. But drums also help people relax and meditate, in Buddhist temples, for example. For many drummers their drum is a friend, a mirror of sound and rhythm in which all their moods can be reflected.

Musicians who create sound effects—thunder, rain, warfare, rumblings of the earth—call on drums to do the job. You can make drums help tell your musical stories and liven up your play.

Give Me Some Skin

Ancient people lived in small groups and hunted animals for their food. For them, skins for drums were readily available. The development of drums thus began early in the history of man because the materials were close at hand.

The musical possibilities of drums are as rich as ever, but obtaining an animal skin is no longer a regular part of everyone's day-to-day life. You'll probably need to invent new ways of making "skins" for the heads of your drums.

Drumheads need to be thin and strong, and they must be stretched tight. If you can get rawhide (tanned leather won't work), you can make an excellent drum. Sometimes music stores that repair drums have rawhide scraps that they will sell cheap.

To stretch rawhide on your drum, cut it first so it overhangs the top of the drum body by about 1 inch all the way around. Soak the hide overnight in water. With leather thongs or strong string lace the wet skin over the ends of your drum as tightly as you possibly can. Let the skin dry. Rawhide shrinks as it dries, so the head of your drum will become very tight.

Canvas is just the opposite of raw-

hide; it shrinks when it is wet. You can make a head of canvas by lacing a piece on your drum while it is dry. When you are ready to play your drum, wet and rub the water into the canvas. The canvas will tighten, and you will be in the drumming business. Thin canvas such as the kind used for building tents is ideal for this type of drumhead.

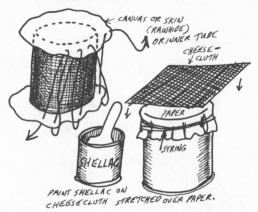

PAINT SHELLAC ON CHEESECLOTH STRETCHED OVER PAPER.

If you are not near a source of inexpensive rawhide or canvas, don't despair. Good drumheads can be made from heavy paper or heavy paper combined with cheesecloth and shellac. If you have thin paper, you may want to glue two or more sheets together. Stretch and secure your paper to the drum body by wrapping it with string or a strong rubber band. Place the cheesecloth over the paper. Secure and stretch it tight also. Shellac the paper and cheesecloth together. When the shellac dries, you should have a good strong-headed drum.

Rubber from tire inner tubes is another material you can use to make drumheads. It is a little awkward to work with, but when you get it laced tight, it makes a nice thumping sound.

Other materials that will work for drumheads include thin plywood, 1/8-inch wood paneling, and poster board. These can be glued to your frame, and sometimes they make great instruments.

CYLINDRICAL DRUMS

CONICAL DRUMS

STAND DRUMS

HOOP DRUMS

A Head Needs a Body

A drumhead without a body or a frame will probably just bend when you hit it. Drum bodies come in lots of shapes and sizes. The cylindrical hollow log and can are very common. Some cylinders are made from mitered sections (like pieces of a pie) of wood glued together. Some are made by wrapping and gluing thin layers of wood around each other until the desired thickness is reached.

Cone-shaped drums are common in Africa and South America. These are often carved of wood or built of clay. Two cones combined, small end to small end, make a narrow-waisted drum common in the Middle and Far East. The narrow-waisted drums are sometimes made so the player can vary the tension on the heads by squeezing the lacings. In Arab and other countries goblet-shaped drums of wood, metal, and clay are played. These drums are often decorated with paintings and inlays.

In Hawaii, Mexico, and parts of Africa people make large standing drums with feet that hold the drums off the ground. Some Native American and Japanese drums are very flat. Some drums from Africa, China, India, and the islands of Oceania have long, narrow, tube shapes. There are kettle-shaped, bowl-shaped, and pot-shaped drums and drums made from gourds, wood, clay, and metal. "Variety" is the word for describing the possibilities in drums. Build a body, tie on a skin, and pick up the beat!

Bongos Tapping in Pairs

Bongos are small Cuban drums that provide dance music throughout Latin America and are also popular in other parts of the world. They are played with sticks, or, more commonly, with

HOW TO MAKE CARPET-TUBE BONGOS

SAW TWO LENGTHS OF CARPET TUBING (ONE 1 FOOT LONG, THE OTHER 8 INCHES OR SO). THE LONGER TUBE WILL PRODUCE A LOWER PITCH.

USE THE END OF THE TUBE FOR A PATTERN AND DRAW TWO CIRCLES ON A PIECE OF ⅛-INCH PANELING OR PLYWOOD. THEN SAW OUT THE CIRCLES FOR THE DRUMHEADS WITH A COPING SAW.

GLUE THE DISKS ON THE TUBES.

TO HOLD THE HEADS ON THE TUBES TAPE THEM WITH MASKING TAPE.

RUN A LINE OF GLUE DOWN ONE SIDE OF YOUR <u>SHORT</u> DRUM AND STAND IT ON ITS HEAD. PRESS THE LONGER DRUM (ALSO STANDING ON ITS HEAD) AGAINST THE GLUE LINE.

TAPE THE TWO DRUMS TOGETHER AND LET THE GLUE DRY. TO MAKE THE DRUMS LOOK NICE AND TO HOLD THEM SECURELY TOGETHER WRAP THEM WITH STRING OR COLORED YARN. FOR FURTHER DECORATIONS USE PAINT, MARKERS, AND YOUR IMAGINATION. TO PLAY YOUR BONGOS HOLD THEM BETWEEN YOUR KNEES AND SLAP THE HEADS WITH YOUR FINGERS AND THUMBS.

the thumbs and fingers of the drummer's hands. Bongos consist of two small drums attached to each other, forming a set.

Carpet stores throw out the large cardboard tubes on which they receive carpet. These tubes are great for making bongos and other drums. Saw off different lengths and glue 1/8-inch plywood or paneling over one end. Remember that you can also make the head from poster board or from paper, cheesecloth, and shellac.

Many drums besides bongos come in sets: the tabla of India, goblet drums of the Ivory Coast, the Arabic naqara,

Yugoslavian talambas, and the orchestral timpani.

The orchestral timpani are among the largest kettledrums, and they are played in tuned sets. Modern models have a pedal that stretches the head and allows the timpanist to play four or five pitches on one instrument. Timpani heads are sensitive to changes in temperature. They expand and contract as these and other conditions vary. The timpanist must continually adjust the tension of the heads to keep them in tune.

With one head or two, be human—start boomin'!

HOW TO MAKE A LION'S ROAR

THIS IS POSITIVELY THE MOST OBNOXIOUS INSTRUMENT IN THIS BOOK.

THE LION'S ROAR IS A TYPE OF FRICTION DRUM. IN AFRICA IT'S MADE FROM A SMALL DRUM WITH A RAWHIDE HEAD, BUT YOU CAN USE A TIN CAN.

SOUP SIZE IS GOOD FOR THE CAN. YOU ALSO NEED A FAIRLY STRONG STRING, A STICK ABOUT SIX INCHES LONG, AND SOME VIOLIN BOW ROSIN.

KNOT

AT THE OTHER END OF THE STRING (18 to 24 INCHES) MAKE A LOOP THAT WILL FIT LOOSELY AROUND THE STICK.

CARVE OR FILE A GROOVE AROUND THE STICK NEAR ONE END. ROSIN THE LOOP AND THE GROOVE.

PUT THE LOOP OVER THE STICK SO IT RESTS IN THE GROOVE.

CHECK TO SEE THAT NO ONE IS IN YOUR WAY. NOW WHIRL THE CAN AND LOVE ♥ ♥ ♥ THAT SOUND!

POKE A HOLE IN THE BOTTOM OF THE EMPTY CAN. SLIP THE STRING THROUGH THE HOLE AND TIE A KNOT SO THE STRING WON'T PULL OUT FROM THE INSIDE OF THE CAN.

THE LION'S ROAR IS ESPECIALLY GOOD AT SCARING EVIL SPIRITS AND MAKING YOU DELIGHTFULLY UNPOPULAR. BY TWISTING THE STICK SLOWLY IN THE LOOP YOU CAN MAKE A GREAT CREAKING! THE SOUND IS PRODUCED WHEN THE LOOP RUBS ON THE STICK. ITS VIBRATION TRAVELS DOWN THE STRING TO THE CAN.

A What?

Drums have some cousins in the membranophone family. They are called mirlitons. Yes, mirlitons. These instruments with a magical sounding name have a membrane that modifies sounds made in some other way. The membrane is usually activated by singing or blowing against it. The kazoo and the eunuch flute are also members of this family.

WAXED PAPER AND COMB KAZOO

KAZOO

Eunuch flutes are played by talking or singing into them. They were played in the seventeenth and eighteenth centuries but are no longer common. The kazoo is a more modern instrument.

The earliest known kazoo was made of wood in 1904. It holds a secure place in jug bands and other music where its razzy, exuberant sound is appreciated.

The kazoo is a tube with a hole cut into its wall. Over the hole is a vibrating membrane. Early kazoos were made of wood, but now they are made of plastic and metal. The metal ones work best. Metal kazoos are made by only one company in the whole world: The Kazoo Company of Eden, New York.

The vibrating membrane of the kazoo is commonly assumed to be made of waxed paper. It is not. It is made from the stomach lining of lambs.

The standard metal kazoo is shaped like a submarine. But it is also made in the shape of a trumpet, trombone, and other instruments. The shape doesn't affect the sound. The shape is mostly for looks.

You can play a kazoo by humming into it, but it works better if you develop a kind of high-pitched singing. The instrument is easy to play and great fun to experiment with. Make a mirliton fast by just folding a piece of waxed paper over a comb. Hold the comb in front of your lips and hum or sing into it. The vibrations from your mouth will shake the paper and make that razzy sound. You and some friends can form a mirliton band almost as fast as you can say, "Membranophone."

Chapter 7
Blowin' in the Winds

Some musical instruments make sound by directly vibrating the air around us. The history of one of these instruments stretches back thousands of years, making it one of the most ancient musical instruments in the world. It is the bull-roarer, an instrument that is believed to date back more than 25,000 years. It was used in early cultures to represent the voice of the wind, thunder, and the cries of spirits and ancestors. The aborigines of Australia and natives of North America, South America, and Africa all play the bull-roarer. There are places in the world where the instrument is still played and enjoyed.

Buzzers and Hummers

The very ancient bull-roarer has a bunch of not-so-ancient relatives still buzzing, whining, and humming in the world. Most people wouldn't even bother to call them instruments, but, like the bull-roarer, they make sounds by spinning into air molecules and knocking them into vibration.

The whine and whistling screams of the electric saws you hear at a construction site are caused by circular blades cutting rapidly through the air. An airplane propeller makes a lower-pitched hum as it whirls and pulls the plane through the molecules of the sky.

Most people call these sounds "noise" and look elsewhere for musical sounds. But not everybody! Some composers are really on the lookout (listenout) for just the right sounds to tell their stories. Some people will try anything just to make music! Bull-roarers and even airplane propellers have found their way into modern musical compositions.

An adventurous, early-twentieth-century American composer, George Antheil, wrote an airplane propeller into one of his pieces. When the propeller was revved up to full speed at the first performance of the composition, it blew music stands over and sent the pages of the composition flying over the heads of the astonished audience —a thrilling, stormy performance.

HOW TO MAKE A BULL-ROARER

WITH A FLAT PIECE OF WOOD AND A STRONG STRING YOU CAN MAKE A BULL-ROARER. BULL-ROARERS COME IN A VARIETY OF SHAPES, SO TUNE IN YOUR IMAGINATION AND DESIGN YOURS.
THE FLAT PIECE OF WOOD NEEDS TO BE LONGER THAN IT IS WIDE. 12 × 3 INCHES IS A GOOD SIZE. THE SHAPE SHOULD BE FAIRLY SYMMETRICAL (SAME BOTH SIDES).

WHIRL

WHITTLE OR SAW THE SHAPE YOU WANT.

DRILL A HOLE NEAR ONE END AND TIE YOUR STRING THROUGH IT. THE STRING SHOULD BE FAIRLY STRONG SO IT WON'T BREAK AS YOU WHIRL THE BOARD THROUGH THE AIR. CHECK TO SEE THAT NOBODY IS IN THE WAY, GRIP THE STRING TIGHT, AND WITH ALL YOUR MIGHT WHIRL THE BOARD THROUGH THE AIR.

THE SOUND OF THE BULL-ROARER IS CAUSED BY THE SPINNING BOARD HITTING AGAINST THE AIR, CAUSING THE AIR TO VIBRATE. IN ORDER TO MAKE A ROAR THE BOARD MUST BE SPINNING AS IT WHIRLS.

IT SOMETIMES TAKES SOME VIGOROUS WHIRLING TO GET THE STRING WOUND UP ENOUGH TO SPIN THE BOARD. IF YOU HAVE A HARD TIME GETTING A SOUND, SLOW DOWN THE WHIRL. LET THE BOARD START SPINNING, THEN WHIRL AWAY.

Aerophones Ready for Takeoff

The bull-roarer and buzz disc-o are the oddball members of a large family of musical instruments called aerophones. No, aerophones are not flying telephones. "Aero" means air, "phone" means sound: they produce sound by the vibration of air. The two oddballs produce sound by vibrating the air around them. Most of the other members of the family—flutes, whistles, horns, and many more—vibrate the air *inside* them.

Most aerophones consist of a tube or vessel that encircles a column of air and in some way makes the air vibrate.

Just like a piece of wood or any other piece of matter, a column of air has a natural rate at which it vibrates. The column of air inside the tube of a flute, a trumpet, or a bassoon is also a chunk of matter. When the player makes a disturbance by blowing in the mouth-

BUZZ DISC-O

YOU CAN EXPERIMENT WITH BUZZING SOUNDS BY MAKING BUZZ-DISCS IN DIFFERENT SIZES AND SHAPES. TO MAKE A BUZZ-DISC FIRST CUT OUT A CIRCLE WITH A 3-OR 4-INCH DIAMETER. DRILL OR PUNCH TWO HOLES ABOUT 1/4 INCH FROM THE CENTER ON OPPOSITE SIDES OF THE CENTER.

THE DISC MAY BE MADE OF A THIN PIECE OF WOOD, HEAVY CARD, A TIN-CAN LID OR A PLASTIC LID. IF YOU USE A TIN LID, BE CAREFUL OF SHARP EDGES.

CUT SOME NOTCHES AROUND THE EDGE OF YOUR DISC. THESE HELP THE DISC "CUT" INTO THE AIR AND DISTURB MOLECULES.

LACE A STRING THAT IS 3 OR 4 FEET LONG THROUGH THE HOLES AND TIE THE ENDS.

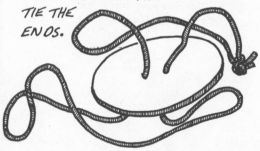

HOOK THE FINGERS OF EACH HAND THROUGH THE LOOP OF STRING AT OPPOSITE SIDES OF THE DISC.

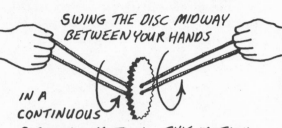

SWING THE DISC MIDWAY BETWEEN YOUR HANDS IN A CONTINUOUS CIRCULAR MOTION. THIS MOTION WILL WIND THE STRING. WHEN THE STRING IS TWISTED ALONG ITS WHOLE LENGTH, PULL YOUR HANDS APART.

THE DISC WILL BEGIN TO SPIN. LOOSEN THE TENSION ON THE STRING AND ALLOW THE SPINNING DISC TO REWIND THE STRING IN THE OPPOSITE DIRECTION. PULL YOUR HANDS APART AGAIN. REPEAT.

WHEN THE DISC IS SPINNING RAPIDLY, IT SHOULD MAKE A BUZZING SOUND.

PLAY WITH THE TONE OF THE DISC BY MAKING MORE NOTCHES OR HOLES IN IT.

NOW YOU'RE BUZZING! TRY SOME DIFFERENT SHAPES.

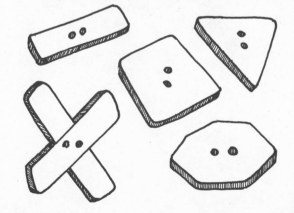

piece, vibrations happening at different rates start traveling through the column of air. Of these many vibrations only the ones that vibrate at the same rate as the natural pitches of the air in the tube can make sound. All the others produce no sound.

The Vessel Flute

Latch on to an empty pop or plastic detergent bottle. You now have a column of air and a container for it. By blowing it properly you can transform the bottle into a musical instrument, the vessel flute.

What makes a flute a flute is that air is made to vibrate with a blow hole. The player directs a stream of air from his mouth across the top of the hole so it bangs into the opposite edge of the hole. As the air rushes against the edge, it is broken up into smaller disturbances. When the rate of vibration of one of these disturbances is the same as the natural rate of vibration (pitch) of the air in the vessel, a sound is produced.

Try it. Hold your bottle so the mouth of it is resting against your lower lip. Blow a stream of air across the mouth of the bottle so it hits the opposite edge. You may get a sound right away. If not, try blowing softer. Then blow harder. Adjust the placement of the bottle and your stream of air until you get a sound. With an empty pop bottle use a firm, fairly slow stream of air. If you are blowing like crazy and getting no sound, you are probably blowing too hard. Once you are able to produce a nice, rich tone, practice it for a while and it will soon become easy.

If you are blowing fairly softly and getting a rich tone, that tone is most likely the fundamental tone for that particular column of air. You can raise the pitch of your instrument by pouring some water into the bottle. As the water goes into the bottle, it forces some of the air out, and the column of air that is left to vibrate is shorter. With a shorter column of air you have to blow slightly harder (faster) to make a strong tone.

To make a tuned set of bottles fill them with different amounts of water until they make just the sounds you want. For lower tones use large bottles and blow very softly. For higher tones use small bottles and blow hard. Take a drink if you're thirsty, but don't forget: it will lower the pitch.

Panpipes

All those water-filled bottles can get to be a little hard to handle, especially for fast tunes. Fortunately Pan, the horned and hooved Greek god of woods and shepherds, invented an improved model. At least he's the one who is credited with the invention of the instrument we call the panpipe.

According to the legend, he had fallen in love with a nymph who could not quite see herself as his partner. As she

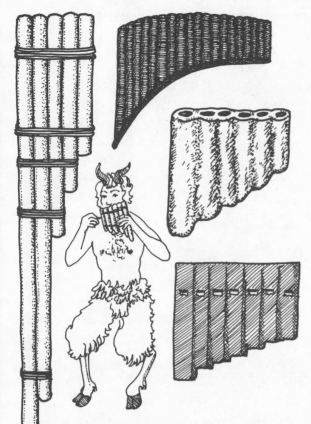

or as many as 25 separate pipes lashed together to make a single instrument. When several panpipe musicians play together, a wide range of notes is possible. Panpipe ensembles (groups) play rich and complicated music. Each musician fits in his or her part like a piece in a large musical puzzle.

The idea behind the panpipe is simple enough. A long column of air has a low pitch. A shorter pipe makes a higher-pitched note. Make pipes the length you want, bind them together, and blow away!

Pipes made of hard, thin materials will generally make louder sounding instruments. The smaller the diameter of the pipes, the easier they are to play, especially for high notes. Lower-pitched pipes usually work better if they have a larger diameter. Experiment with different materials and see which one sounds best to you.

Musical instruments can be tuned in all sorts of ways, and are. Tuning is really up to the people who make the instruments. They choose the pitches their instruments will produce. "They," in this case, means you.

Flutes Take
the Harmonic Series

It is possible to produce more than one pitch from a particular length of tube. When you blow softly on one of the pipes of your panpipe, you produce its fundamental pitch. This tone has a vibration that completes one cycle within the length of the tube. If you blow hard and create a vibration that is twice as fast as the fundamental, you will get another tone. The higher-pitched tone is the first harmonic. If you blow even harder, you might produce a third tone. The air would now be vibrating three times faster than the fundamental. Three complete waves would form within the length of

was fleeing from his affections, a thoughtful, protecting deity turned her into a reed (a hollow-stemmed plant). Heartbroken, Pan used this reed to make the first syrinx, a Greek panpipe, and played it to soothe his broken heart. How the nymph felt about this we'll never know. People have been enjoying the music of panpipes for thousands of years.

Panpipes are sets of tubes of different lengths that are joined together like the logs of a raft, or in a bunch. Sound is produced by blowing across the top of the tubes, just as you did to make your bottle sound. The tubes are usually stopped (plugged up) at the lower end, and they have no finger holes. Examples of these instruments have been found in most parts of the world. They have been made of materials as varied as cane, clay, bones, stone, wood, metal, and plastic.

A panpipe may have as few as 3 or 4

HOW TO MAKE PANPIPES
IN THE KEY OF C

TO MAKE A PANPIPE THAT WILL PLAY IN THE KEY OF C YOU NEED SOME ½ INCH HARD PLASTIC PIPE (PVC). YOU CAN BUY A 10-FOOT LENGTH AT A HARDWARE STORE FOR ABOUT A DOLLAR. FOR SOME MYSTERIOUS REASON ½-INCH PLASTIC PIPE HAS AN INSIDE DIAMETER OF ABOUT 5/8 INCH. YOU NEED TO KNOW THIS WHEN YOU GET MATERIAL FOR PLUGS. DOWELS CUT INTO 1- OR 2-INCH-LONG CHUNKS, CORKS, OR PLUGS YOU WHITTLE FROM A BRANCH MAKE GOOD PLUGS. THE PLUGS MUST FIT AIRTIGHT.

PVC

MAKE THEM AIRTIGHT BY COATING THEM WITH A LITTLE GLUE OR TIGHTLY WRAPPING THE JOINT WITH TAPE WHERE THE PLUG MEETS THE TUBE.

MAKE A MEASURING STICK THAT EASILY FITS INSIDE YOUR TUBE. MAKE MARKS ALONG THE STICK AT 12½, 11⅛, 10, 9¼, 8⅛, 7⅛, 6¼, AND 6⅛ INCHES FROM ONE END.

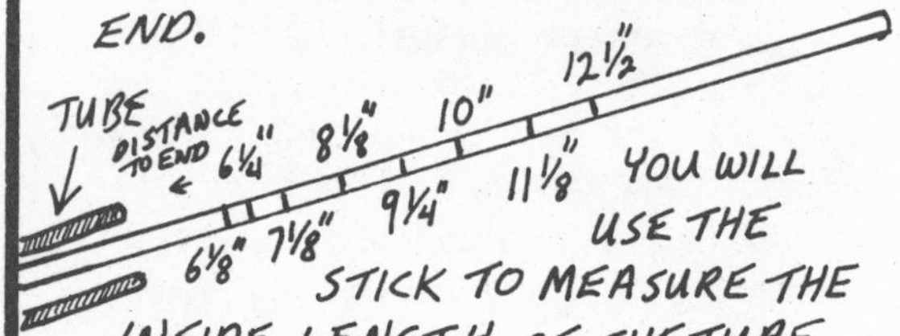

TUBE ↓ DISTANCE TO END 6¼" 8⅛" 10" 12½ 6⅛" 7⅛" 9¼" 11⅛ YOU WILL USE THE STICK TO MEASURE THE INSIDE LENGTH OF THE TUBE FROM ITS TOP EDGE TO THE PLUG.

CUT YOUR PIPE WITH A SAW OR HACKSAW INTO LENGTHS ABOUT 1 INCH LONGER THAN THE MARKS ON YOUR STICK, ONE PIPE FOR EACH MARK. THIS WILL GIVE YOU SOME ROOM IN THE TUBE TO PUT IN AND ADJUST YOUR PLUG.

PUT IN THE PLUGS. SHOVE THEM TO JUST THE RIGHT PLACE USING YOUR STICK TO MEASURE.

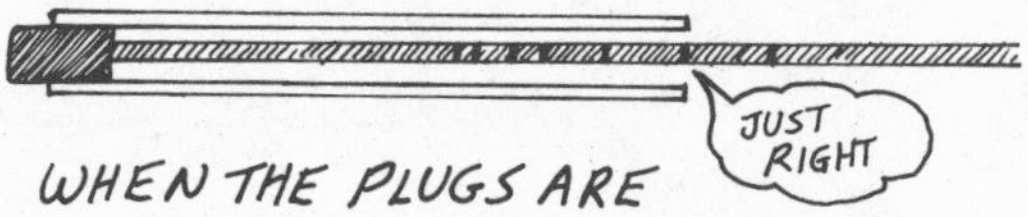

JUST RIGHT

WHEN THE PLUGS ARE ALL IN PLACE, TIE THE TUBES TOGETHER LIKE A RAFT. SOME STICKS AND STRING HELP HOLD THE TUBES IN PLACE. SO DOES GLUE BETWEEN TUBES.

HOW TO MAKE A SIMPLE FLUTE

TO MAKE A SIMPLE FLUTE YOU NEED A PIECE OF TUBING. IT SHOULD BE CLOSED AT ONE END. IF THE TUBE IS HOLLOW ALL THE WAY THROUGH, YOU WILL NEED TO MAKE AN AIRTIGHT PLUG FOR ONE END.

DRILL A HOLE FOR A BLOW HOLE 2 INCHES FROM THE CLOSED END. MAKE THE HOLE 3/8 OR 1/2 INCH IN DIAMETER. ITS SIDES SHOULD BE SMOOTH AND CLEAN.

BLOW HOLE

A ROLLED-UP PIECE OF SANDPAPER DOES WONDERS SMOOTHING THE HOLE.

HOLD THE BLOW HOLE TO YOUR LOWER LIP WITH THE TUBE GOING TO ONE SIDE.

PLACE YOUR FINGERS ALONG THE TUBE SO THE PADS OF YOUR FINGERTIPS ARE ON THE TUBE AND RELAXED. MARK THESE SPOTS FOR FINGER HOLES WITH A MARKER OR PENCIL. AT THESE POINTS DRILL FINGER HOLES THAT ARE AT LEAST 1/8 INCH IN DIAMETER. THE NUMBER OF HOLES YOU DRILL IS UP TO YOU.

CONSIDER THE NUMBER OF FINGERS YOU HAVE TO COVER THEM WITH BEFORE YOU DRILL TOO MANY.

YOU CAN RAISE THE PITCH OF A FLUTE'S NOTE A LITTLE BY ENLARGING THE FINGER HOLES. WHEN THE HOLES ARE LARGER, MORE AIR PASSES THROUGH, AND THE AIR IN THE TUBE VIBRATES AS IF THE TUBE WERE SHORTER.

TO PLAY YOUR FLUTE REST THE TUBE AGAINST YOUR LOWER LIP WITH THE BLOW HOLE FACING UP. AIM A THIN, STEADY STREAM OF AIR SO IT HITS THE FAR EDGE OF THE HOLE. BLOW SOFT AND HARD UNTIL YOU GET A TONE. YOU MAY NEED TO ADJUST THE ANGLE OF THE HOLE TO YOUR MOUTH. THIS FLUTE IS FOR YOUR ENJOYMENT — STAY RELAXED AS YOU LEARN TO MAKE IT SOUND. IF YOU BECOME TOO FRUSTRATED, PUT IT ASIDE AND TRY AGAIN ANOTHER TIME. YOU NEED TO BLOW A LITTLE HARDER TO PRODUCE THE NOTES ON A SHORT FLUTE. IF YOU MAKE A VERY LONG FLUTE, 2 OR 3 FEET, YOU MUST BLOW VERY SOFTLY AND STEADILY.

the tube. On some wind instruments you can play five or more notes of the harmonic series with one length of tubing.

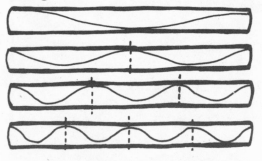

Some people are always looking for ways to do more with less. Thousands of years ago things were much the same way. Someone discovered it is possible to create the effect of a set of pipes by drilling holes in the side of a single long pipe. When you cover the holes, one fundamental pitch and its harmonics can be blown. By opening a hole at the lower end of the tube, a new fundamental and its harmonics become possible. With another hole open, the tube is effectively shortened and another set of tones is possible.

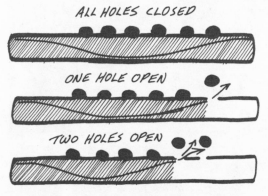

ALL HOLES CLOSED

ONE HOLE OPEN

TWO HOLES OPEN

Most flutes are made with one piece of tubing and one blow hole through which the player can disturb the air in the tube. They produce a wide range of sounds. Tones can be quickly changed as the player opens and closes holes in the tube and as she changes the speed of the stream of air at the blow hole.

Theobald Boehm's Flute

Some people spend their lives trying to build a better mousetrap. Theobald Boehm (pronounced bo-eem) spent his life trying to make a better flute. He was very successful. In 1847 he invented a flute that has been the standard of excellence for over 130 years.

When Boehm was born in Munich, Bavaria (now West Germany), in 1793, most of the flute players in his part of the world were playing flutes made of wood. These instruments had finger holes that were hard to reach. Their tone was often weak and inaccurate, especially when compared to the flutes used in bands and orchestras today.

Boehm acquired his lifelong love of the flute as a child. He began his flute career playing the flageolet, a whistle flute. When it no longer suited him, he took up the flute. At age 16 he made his first flute by copying a four-key model lent him by a friend. A professional musician heard him playing one day, offered him lessons, and in a few years he was dazzling audiences with his skill as a flutist.

Boehm was a goldsmith and used his shop and tools to make flutes until he became a fulltime musician. In 1828 he started his own flute factory. His goal was to make the best possible flute. The first model he manufactured won wide acceptance for its tone and beauty. Boehm was a skilled musician, craftsman, and inventor. He studied acoustics, the science of sound, then applied what he had learned to his flutemaking. He continued making improvements on his instruments throughout his life.

His masterpiece, a silver flute made in 1847, had keys that made it easy to play. The fingerings were comfortable and logical. The holes were made and placed so the flute produced strong, accurate tones throughout its length. This instrument was not recognized during Boehm's lifetime as the unique invention it was, but modern flutes that are manufactured today are all copies of his instrument.

Let's Hear It for Whistles

Playing a flute with a blow hole takes a special knack. Some people are very good at aiming a stream of air at the edge of a hole. They can easily produce a sound. Some try and try and it just never works. But flute failures can be whistles whizzes. The whistle is a little harder to make than a blow-hole flute, but anybody who can blow can make one sound.

All the tube and finger-hole stuff that applies to flutes also applies to whistles. The big difference is how the disturbance is made. The whistle has a mouthpiece that directs a thin stream of air against a sharp edge, causing the air to vibrate. Once the mouthpiece is properly made, it is easy to play. No special aim is necessary. Perhaps this is why whistles have worldwide popularity.

Archeologists have found ancient whistles made from human and animal bones. The next time you have chicken or turkey, save a leg bone. If you boil it,

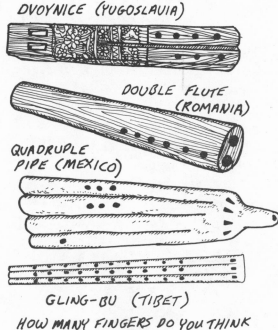

DVOYNICE (YUGOSLAVIA)

DOUBLE FLUTE (ROMANIA)

QUADRUPLE PIPE (MEXICO)

GLING-BU (TIBET)

HOW MANY FINGERS DO YOU THINK TIBETANS HAVE?

then scrape out the soft insides with a thick wire, you will have a bone tube with which you can make a whistle. Whistles are also made of wood, clay, metal, animal horns, gourds, plastic, and paper.

The people of Slovakia play a wooden whistle that is about 6 feet long. It is called the fujara. Even bigger are the pipes on pipe organs. These large whistles are sometimes 10 to 20 feet long and need to be blown by a machine.

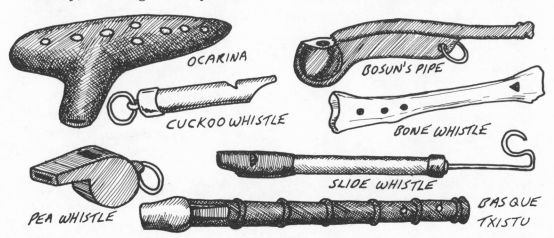

OCARINA

CUCKOO WHISTLE

PEA WHISTLE

BOSUN'S PIPE

BONE WHISTLE

SLIDE WHISTLE

BASQUE TXISTU

DISTURBING PARTS OF WHISTLES

THE DISTURBANCE THAT MAKES SOUND POSSIBLE IN A WHISTLE IS MADE BY A STREAM OF AIR DIRECTED AT A SHARP EDGE CALLED THE LIP. AT THE LIP THE STREAM OF AIR IS SLICED INTO LITTLE, TURBULENT EDDY OR SPIRAL MOVEMENTS, WHICH START TREMORS TRAVELING DOWN THE COLUMN OF AIR INSIDE THE TUBE.

TO MAKE A WHISTLE YOU NEED A TUBE, A PLUG, AND SOME TOOLS. THE ½-INCH PLASTIC PIPE YOU USED FOR THE PANPIPE, A CHUNK OF BAMBOO, OR A PIECE OF GARDEN HOSE ARE POSSIBLE TUBES.

SAW A NOTCH ALMOST (BUT NOT QUITE) HALFWAY THROUGH THE TUBE ABOUT 1 INCH FROM THE END WHERE YOU INTEND TO BLOW.

SAW, SHAVE WITH A KNIFE, OR FILE WITH A FAIRLY SMOOTH HALF-ROUND FILE A SLANT ABOUT 45°

UNTIL THE HALF-CIRCLE-SHAPED HOLE IS ABOUT ¼-INCH ACROSS.

THE BLADE OR LIP SHOULD BE SMOOTH AND SHARP. SOME PEOPLE HAVE SHARP TONGUES. WHISTLES HAVE SHARP LIPS!

THE WINDWAY IS THE CHANNEL THAT DIRECTS THE AIR FROM YOUR MOUTH AT THE LIP OF THE WHISTLE. YOU CAN MAKE A PLUG-STYLE WINDWAY WITH A CHUNK OF WOOD (BALSA, A BRANCH, OR A DOWEL), RUBBER STOPPER, OR CORK THAT SLIPS FIRMLY INTO YOUR TUBE. TO GET THE PLUG IN AND OUT AS YOU ARE WORKING ON IT, USE A PUSHROD MADE FROM A LONG STICK.

THE PLUG SHOULD BE AN INCH OR SO LONG. CUT A SLANT SO THE TOP SURFACE OF THE PLUG IS FLAT, SMOOTH, AND SLANTED.

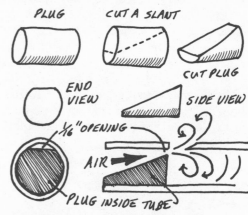

SLIDE THE FINISHED PLUG (THICK END FIRST) SO THE WIDE END OF THE PLUG IS EVEN WITH THE FLAT EDGE OF THE NOTCH.

BLOW <u>SOFTLY</u>. YOU SHOULD GET A SOUND.

(CONTINUED ON NEXT PAGE)

WHISTLES (CONTINUED)

IF YOU DO NOT GET A SOUND, BLOW SOFTER. IF NONE, PUSH THE PLUG IN A <u>LITTLE</u> AND TRY AGAIN. STILL NONE? PUSH THE PLUG BACK A <u>LITTLE</u> WITH YOUR PUSH ROD. IF YOU STILL DON'T GET A GOOD TONE, CHECK THESE THINGS:

① IF THE SLANT ON THE PLUG IS SHALLOW, MAKE IT STEEPER.

TOO SHALLOW   GOOD SLANT

② IS AIR GETTING TO THE LIP? IF NOT, FILE, CARVE, OR SAND THE SURFACE A LITTLE LOWER.

NO AIR   ENOUGH ROOM

③ IS TOO MUCH AIR GETTING THROUGH?

TOO MUCH AIR

MAKE A NEW PLUG.

④ IS THE TOP EDGE OF THE PLUG SHARP? IS THE LIP?

CLEAN AND SHARP

DULL

CLEAN UP AND SHARPEN. MAKE A NEW PLUG OR NOTCH IF YOU NEED TO.

⑤ IS THE PLUG SO LOOSE IT MOVES WHEN YOU BLOW? SOMETIMES YOU CAN GLUE IT OR YOU MAY HAVE TO MAKE

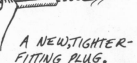

A NEW, TIGHTER-FITTING PLUG.

NOT ALL WHISTLES HAVE A SLANTED-PLUG WINDWAY. THE RECORDER HAS A CHANNEL CARVED INTO THE SIDE OF THE MOUTHPIECE WALL. SOME WHISTLES HAVE A WINDWAY MADE OF A SMALL TUBE THAT IS GLUED ON THE OUTSIDE SO IT POINTS THE AIR AT THE EDGE OF THE HOLE OR LIP.

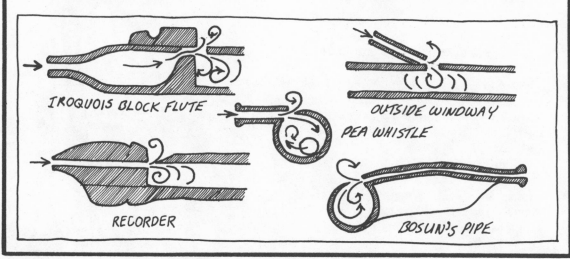

IROQUOIS BLOCK FLUTE

OUTSIDE WINDWAY PEA WHISTLE

RECORDER

BOSUN'S PIPE

Bodies to Whistle At

Whistle mouthpieces are usually attached to a body of some shape and size. Many whistles have tubular bodies with finger holes running down their sides to change the pitch. There are also vessel whistles that have a clay pot or a gourd for a body instead of a tube. The most popular is the ocarina, also known as the sweet potato.

Sometimes whistles are arranged in groups that look like panpipes. The dvojachka of Slovakia and the dvoynice of Yugoslavia are each made of two whistles and two tubes and are played at the same time by the same player. Multiple whistles with three or four tubes are played in Mexico and Tibet.

FELT OR LEATHER

The slide whistle has a plunger that the player slides in and out to change the pitch. You can make one of these easily by not drilling holes in your whistle tube. Instead, you need a stick with a piece of leather or felt attached to the end of it to make a plunger. Stick the plunger in your tube, then blow and slide away!

An interesting, inexpensive instrument known as a nose flute, or humanatone, can be purchased at a music store. Play it by blowing through your nose! Your mouth is the resonat-ing vessel, and you change the pitch by moving your jaws, tongue, and lips.

Double-beating Reeds

Follow the instructions on the opposite page to make a double-beating reed. Both the top and bottom rapidly open and shut as you blow. A train of pulses of air passes between them and makes the air vibrate. Double-beating reeds made from a dandelion or drinking straw work the same way as the reeds of the oboe, bassoon, and several other instruments.

The names alone of some of these other instruments are enough to stir even a sluggish imagination. A group of double-reed instruments called shawms includes: the zurla, sopile, surnaj, tiple, piffaro, tarogato, bombarde, zurna, shanai, alghaita, sona, sralay, and pi nai. Shawms have a simple double reed attached to a tubular body that is equipped with finger holes. It has a loud sound and is especially suited to outdoor playing. These instruments are common in Europe, Asia, and parts of Africa.

You can easily make a shawm by taping your drinking-straw reed into the end of a piece of plastic pipe. Hold

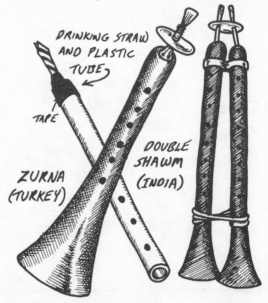

DRINKING STRAW AND PLASTIC TUBE

TAPE

ZURNA (TURKEY)

DOUBLE SHAWM (INDIA)

100

A REEDING LESSON

Q.   WHAT DOES A DANDELION STEM HAVE IN COMMON WITH A DRINKING STRAW?

A.   EACH CAN BE MADE INTO A MUSICAL INSTRUMENT.

A DANDELION ROARS

FIND A DANDELION WITH A NICE LONG STEM. BREAK THE STEM OFF NEAR THE GROUND AND PINCH THE FLOWER FROM THE OTHER END.

TRIM THE END WHERE THE FLOWER WAS WITH YOUR FRONT TEETH. MAKE IT NICE AND STRAIGHT. SMASH THIS END BETWEEN YOUR THUMB AND FIRST FINGER.

3/4 INCH

PLACE THE SMASHED END INTO THE CAVITY OF YOUR MOUTH. GRIP THE STEM WITH YOUR LIPS SO THAT ANY AIR THAT ESCAPES FROM YOUR MOUTH IS FORCED TO GO THROUGH THE STEM. BE CAREFUL NOT TO CRUSH THE STEM WITH YOUR LIPS. NOW BLOW. YOU SHOULD GET A BUZZING SOUND. BY CUPPING YOUR HANDS AROUND THE OPEN END OF THE STEM AND WIGGLING THEM YOU CAN VARY THE SOUND AND MAKE IT LOUDER.

THE SINGING STRAW

GET A PAPER OR PLASTIC DRINKING STRAW. SMASH ONE END BETWEEN YOUR THUMB AND FOREFINGER.

WITH SCISSORS CUT THE FLATTENED END TO MAKE A POINT. PUT THE FLATTENED, POINTED END INTO YOUR MOUTH CAVITY. CLOSE YOUR LIPS FIRMLY AROUND THE SHAFT OF THE STRAW AND BLOW. YOU MIGHT HAVE TO BLOW HARD TO MAKE IT SOUND. PLASTIC STRAWS ARE SOMETIMES HARD TO FLATTEN. TO MAKE THE END GOOD AND FLAT YOU CAN CREASE IT BY PULLING IT THROUGH YOUR CLOSED FRONT TEETH. CUT THE STRAW SHORTER TO RAISE THE PITCH. TAPE ON A TUBE TO LOWER IT.

the reed inside the cavity of your mouth and blow hard. If you make finger holes in the side of your tube, your shawm will make several tones.

In the sixteenth century some shawmlike instruments were developed that were more suited to indoor playing. These instruments had reed caps that covered the reed. The caps make a wind chamber that is easy to blow. The courtaut, cornemuse, crumhorn, curtal, sclalmei, sordone, and rauschpfeife are members of this gentle, buzzing group. These instruments are still played today by people who are interested in music of the baroque period.

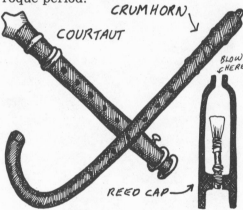

CRUMHORN

COURTAUT

BLOW HERE

REED CAP

The Oboe and Bassoon

The orchestral oboe looks a lot like a clarinet. They are about the same size, covered with keys, and usually made of a dark hardwood like rosewood or granadilla, a very hard wood from the West Indies. The oboe, however, has a double-beating reed, which is made of a special cane that grows only in the Var district in southern France. Oboe players spend a lot of time very carefully making their reeds so they are just right. Slight differences in reed thickness and length make quite a difference in how the instrument sounds.

The oboe has a warm, penetrating tone. Of all the instruments in the or-

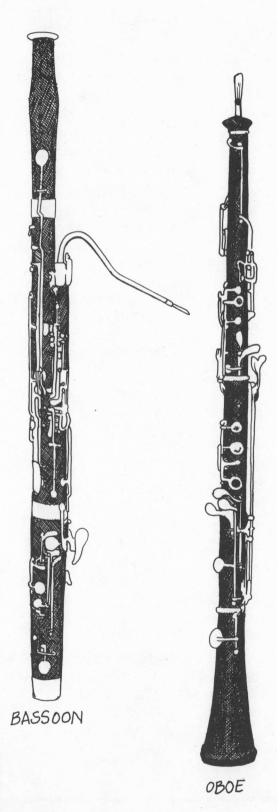

BASSOON

OBOE

CLARINET REEDS

REED CUT INTO SIDE OF TUBE

REED ATTACHED TO SIDE OF TUBE

IDIOGLOTTAL   HETEROGLOTTAL

chestra, its sound is probably most like the human voice. It is one of the most difficult instruments in the orchestra to play well. On top of that, the musician must constantly make new reeds.

The nearest big brother to the oboe is the English horn. This instrument is also called the alto oboe. The English horn can be recognized by the bulb on its lower end. It plays a lower range of notes than the oboe.

The third instrument in the double-reed section of the orchestra is the bassoon. The red-stained tube of maple wood, of which the bassoon's body is made, encloses a column of air 8 feet long! To make it easier to play, this long tube is folded in half. Bassoons can play either the bass or tenor part.

The largest of the double-reed instruments in the symphony orchestra is the contrabassoon. It plays very low notes. The tones it can play are sometimes so low they cause the floor to vibrate in resonance. Its wooden tube is about 16 feet long and is folded into three sections.

Clarinets

Clarinets are wind instruments in which the vibration is produced by a single, rapidly beating reed. The reed is a tongue either cut from or attached to a cylindrical tube. When blown, the reed vibrates and breaks the stream of air from the player's mouth into a series of rapid little pulses. The column of air in the tube of the instrument resonates with some of these pulses to make sound.

The Orchestral Clarinet

Around 1700 a German instrument maker, J. C. Denner, made some improvements in a single-reed instrument called the chalumeau. The orchestral clarinet was born. Denner's clarinet had a separate mouthpiece and some keys that enabled it to play higher notes. In the 1840s the Boehm system of keys was adapted to the clarinet, and the instrument has remained much the same since then.

Actually, the clarinets are a family of six orchestral instruments. The three smaller ones are usually made of hard plastic or granadilla, the very hard wood from the West Indies. The three larger members of the family have a bent and flared metal part (the bell) at the lower, open end of the tube and metal neck crooks (bends near the mouthpiece). Even though different

members of the family produce different sounds, their keys are arranged the same, so a clarinet player can play all the instruments of the family without having to learn new fingerings.

A brassy relative of the clarinet is the saxophone. It was invented about 1840 by Adolphe Sax. He actually developed a family of 14 saxophones, but only 8 are commonly made today. Saxophones are made of brass instead of wood, and they have a cone-shaped bore (inside shape). The saxophone has become especially popular with jazz and band musicians.

The clarinet and saxophone look amazing with all their keys. In some ways they really are amazing machines. They are also fairly simple to understand. Just as in the flute and the whistle, the body of the instrument encloses a column of air. The disturbance created at the mouthpiece sends pulses traveling through the column. Some of these vibrations help the air in the tube to sound. The holes and the keys allow the player to select the sounds she wants to produce.

For a warm smooth sound or for razzmatazz jazz, the clarinet is king!

YOU CAN MAKE A SIMPLE CLARINET FROM A CARDBOARD CANDY BOX. YOU NEED THE TYPE WITH A LID THAT IS RECLOSABLE.

ZIPS

WHEN THE BOX HAS BEEN EMPTIED, CLOSE THE LID. PLACE THE END OF THE BOX INTO YOUR MOUTH AND BLOW. YOU CAN VARY THE TONE BY CUPPING YOUR HANDS OVER THE BOX AND WIGGLING THEM.

The clarinet probably originated in ancient Egypt. Most early clarinets were developed in North Africa, Europe, and South America. These are places where the cane suited for making reeds naturally grew. Once the material met the idea, many different varieties of clarinet were invented.

The simplest clarinets are made from a single stalk of hollow cane. A reed is cut in the side, and perhaps a few finger holes are drilled along the length of the tube.

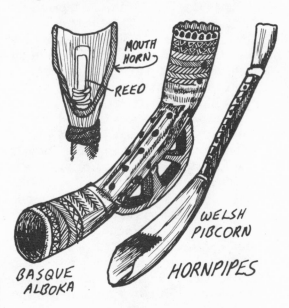

MOUTH HORN

REED

BASQUE ALBOKA

WELSH PIBCORN

HORNPIPES

The hornpipe is another simple clarinet. In its simplest form a stalk of cane with a reed cut into the side is inserted into the narrow end of an animal horn. The horn helps amplify the sound of the reed. The Basque alboka from northern Spain has two cane pipes attached to a wooden handle with horns on both ends. One of the horns is for blowing into; the other is for amplifying the sound. The pibcorn comes from Wales. It has a single pipe with a smaller mouth horn on one end and a larger resonating horn on the other.

The tiktiri, the instrument played by Indian snake charmers, has two cane

104

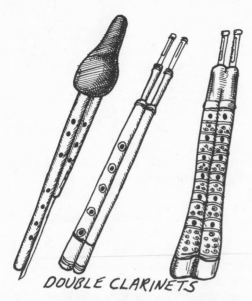

DOUBLE CLARINETS

pipes fitted into a gourd into which the player blows. The diple surle from Yugoslavia has two wooden pipes fitted into a wooden mouth horn against which the player seals his mouth to blow.

Other double clarinets, such as the arghul of Egypt, have no horn. The largest of the double clarinets is the urua. It is played in the rituals of the Camayura people of Brazil. This instrument is made of two unequal lengths of cane. Each one has a reed mounted inside. The longer one, which is 6 or 7 feet long, is considered the male. The shorter is considered the female.

When more than one pipe comprises a clarinet, sometimes one functions as a drone. A drone plays one steady tone. Sometimes two or even three of the pipes are used to play the melody.

If That's Your Bag

Do you ever want to do two things at once? Sometimes that impulse can get you into trouble. But other times you can do remarkable things. The spirit that's needed to carry on two (or more!) things at once probably helped invent the bagpipes. A bagpipe player can play several different pipes at the same time. These instruments have both a beauty and a madness all their own. People usually feel strongly about bagpipes—they either really like them or they really don't.

Bagpipes, called "pipes" by their friends, provide music for listening, dancing, ceremonies, and even for wars. It was probably a bagpipe that the Pied Piper of Hamlin played to rid that city of its rats. Where the idea of bagpipes began no one knows for sure. The Romans used them to pipe the glory of Rome. Pipers have piped for soldiers on their way to, and even during, battles. Sometimes pipes were played to frighten the enemy. In war and peace bagpipes stir something of the joy and wildness that lives inside people.

The highland pipes played by the kilted pipers of Scotland are a familiar instrument. These loud pipes are suited for parades, parties, and celebrations where loud and wild music is appreciated. Across Europe, Asia, and North Africa there are lots of other kinds of bagpipes too. Some of these have a different personality; they play quiet and pleasant songs.

What all bagpipes have in common is a bag, usually made of animal skin. The player blows through a mouthpipe, whose job is not to make sound but to inflate the bag. Not all bagpipes are inflated by human breath. Some, like the French musette and the Irish Union pipe, are blown up with bellows. The bellows is an air pump that is powered by the player's arm.

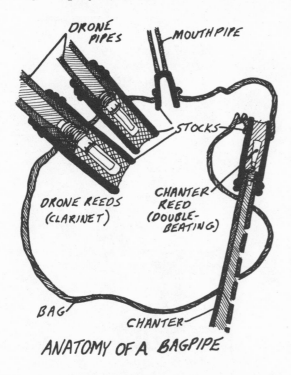

ANATOMY OF A BAGPIPE

The bag makes it possible for the player to play several separate pipes at the same time. The pipes, each of which has its own single- or double-beating reed, are fastened to the bag. As the player squeezes the bag with his arm, the air in the bag is forced through the reeds of all the pipes at once and causes them all to sound.

Some of the pipes are drones that play one steady tone. Sometimes several drones are tuned to play together to produce a sound called a chord. A drone pipe usually has a clarinet reed.

The chanter, which has finger holes drilled in its side, is the pipe on which the melody is played. Some chanters have single reeds and some have double reeds. Chanters are made of wood, plastic, cane, bone, or metal.

Playing While You Work

You can make a bagpipe sound with a vacuum cleaner or any other machine that has a motor that makes a continuous tone. A friend could do this with you. While the motor drones (makes its steady noise), you begin to hum or sing. When you are in tune with the drone, the vibrations your voice is making will feel very pleasant. Try doing whole melodies with your voice as the drone drones on. This is a good way to make your work fun.

Music has been used by all sorts of people to make work more pleasant. Sailors used to sing as they hoisted their sails; it helped them maintain a safe rhythm in their work. Crews of African fishing boats sing as they row. The gandy dancers who worked on the early American railroads sang special songs as they straightened the tracks. Modern factories use music to help their workers be more productive and stay happy. Music not only helps workers play, it also helps workers work.

Trumpets and Horns
Are a Blast

Musicologists, people who study music, separate horns from trumpets by their shapes. Horns usually have a cone-shaped body and tend to be curved. Trumpets have a cylindrical shaped body and are usually straight.

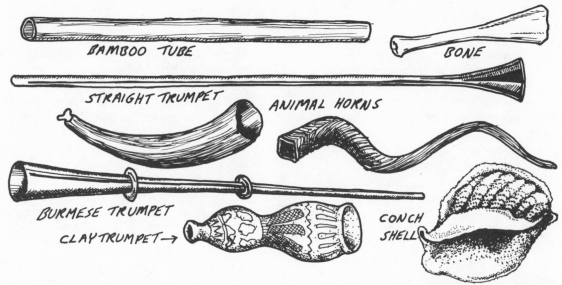

BAMBOO TUBE

BONE

STRAIGHT TRUMPET

ANIMAL HORNS

BURMESE TRUMPET

CLAY TRUMPET →

CONCH SHELL

The first horns and trumpets were probably made from animal horns or perhaps from hollowed-out bones. In some tropical climates bamboo tubes were used, and on the islands of the south seas, such as Hawaii, spiral-shaped seashells became horns and trumpets. These early instruments allowed people to send signals distances that were a little too far for shouting. Different cultures developed special codes of tones and rhythms to communicate important messages. The instruments also found their way into the ceremonies and play of primitive people.

Since animals willing to contribute their horns to musicians were sometimes hard to find, musicians began to look elsewhere for hornmaking materials. People make horns of clay, leather, bark, armadillo tails, and even from human bones.

The aborigine people of Australia play an instrument called the didgeridoo. It's a very simple trumpet made of a hollowed-out, straight eucalyptus tree branch about 4 feet long. The instrument is stored in mud to keep it moist because moistness affects the tone. Players blow and sing through the tube to make it sound. The best

players are able to make very complex and beautiful music on this simple instrument. When the ceremonies for which it is played are finished, the didgeridoo is again buried carefully in wet mud for safekeeping.

DIDGERIDOO
(EUCALYPTUS WOOD TUBE)

Pygmies who live in the Ituri forest in Africa play a simple trumpet in their ceremonies. Theirs, also, is a straight hollow tube. They call it the molimo; it has special powers, and its voice is the voice of the forest. The molimo comes on special occasions and sings to the people in the night. When the molimo is brought to the village and played, the women and children must stay safely inside their huts. The molimo trumpet is stored in a stream deep in the forest when it is not in use, and only the men know where it sleeps. Like the player of the didgeridoo, the molimo player not only blows but also sings and shouts through the tube.

Some people like to make instruments louder; others like to make them bigger. The people of some tribes in South America make large trumpets of bark wound in a spiral. Priests in Burma play long metal instruments that are so long two men are needed to carry each instrument. The longest simple trumpet is the alphorn of the Swiss Alps. Made from a hollow tree, it is often 12 or more feet long.

To make an alphorn a young, straight spruce tree with a bend near the ground is cut down. It is sawed in half lengthwise. The insides are carved out so only a thin shell of wood remains. The two sides are then fitted and glued back together and wound with leather. The longest alphorn ever made—43 feet—was made in 1976 in Switzerland.

You Toot Too

With any kind of tubing you can make a simple trumpet. A length of garden hose, cardboard tubes, plastic or metal pipe, any sort of tube will work. The diameter of the tube must not be so large that you can't seal it up with your mouth. If the diameter is too small, as well, you will have trouble making the tube sound.

To play, you close your lips, stretch them back against your teeth, and blow. You may have to adjust the tension of your lips to make the right vibration for your length of tube. Shorter tubes usually need tighter lips. The longer tubes are sounded with more relaxed lips.

To make a long horn, you can add one tube onto another, then another, and another, until you have the length you want. When you add tubes to one another, they must fit tight so there are no air leaks at the joints. A wrap of tape usually does the job, or you can wrap a narrower tube with a thick string or rag and fit it into a tube with a larger diameter.

Making a Long Horn Short

Long, straight horns are just great for people who never go anywhere. For people on the move they are just too awkward. Instrument makers began

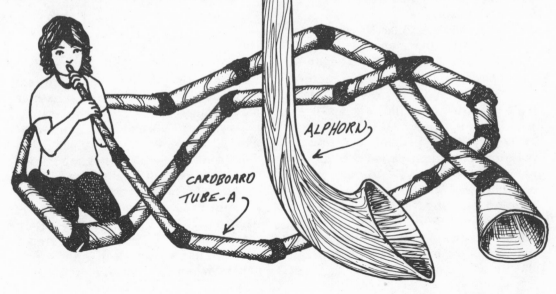

ALPHORN

CARDBOARD TUBE-A

108

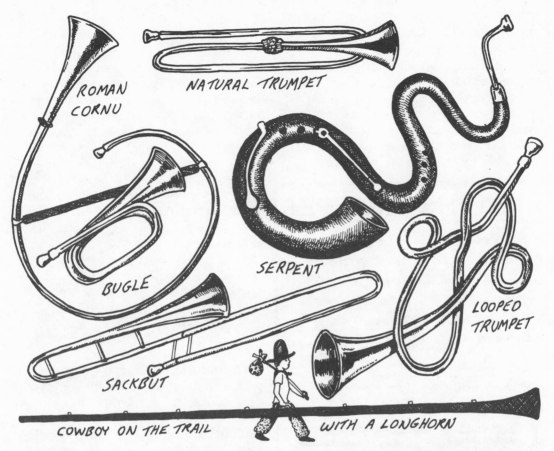

ROMAN CORNU

NATURAL TRUMPET

BUGLE

SERPENT

LOOPED TRUMPET

SACKBUT

COWBOY ON THE TRAIL WITH A LONGHORN

long ago to look for ways to enjoy the benefits of a long tube and the convenience of a short one. The solution they came up with was to bend the tubes. Now this solution may seem obvious to you, but for people who had never seen a curved tube it was quite a new idea. Bending a tube of wood or even of metal is no easy job. Wood breaks easily and metal crimps when it is bent.

Curved wooden tubes are made by sawing out the desired shape. The shape is then sliced in half. The insides are carved out and the two sides are put back together. Often a thin coating of leather is sewn over the tube to hold it together, and to make it airtight and strong.

To bend metal tubes without crimping them they must be filled with lead or sand. The ends of the tube are plugged, the tube is heated, then the tube is gradually bent. The material inside the tube keeps it from crimping as it is bent. Instead of crimping, the metal is forced to stretch. When the bending is done, the sand is poured out to leave a hollow curved tube. When lead is used, it is melted out. Using these methods, you can bend horns and trumpets into all kinds of shapes. A look at a book about old musical instruments will let you see just how imaginative some oldtime instrument makers were.

Out of the experimentation with shapes emerged an instrument called the natural trumpet about 1500. It was about 7 feet long and folded over to make one long loop. This was the form it kept for the next 300 years.

To play different notes on a simple trumpet the player adjusts his lips and blows harder or softer. With any particular length of tube a limited number of notes are possible. These are the fundamental and its harmonics. With some trumpets as many as five separate notes are possible. These are the notes heard in bugle calls. Tunes such as taps, reveille, and the post call heard at horseraces are bugle calls.

In the 1400s the sackbut was invented. This instrument had a U-shaped sliding tube that the player could move to change the length of the column of air inside it. This instrument is still played today. You would recognize the design, but the name has been changed from sackbut to trombone. The slide of the trombone can be moved rapidly to a new position. Each time it is moved different tones (a new fundamental and several harmonics) are possible.

You can build a sliding trumpet with two pieces of tubing. One piece must fit into the other. Blow on the end of the smaller tube and slide the larger one.

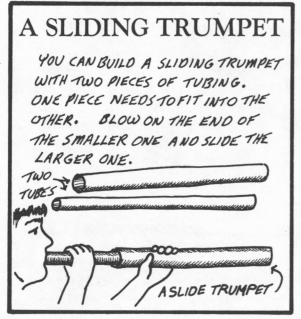

A SLIDING TRUMPET

YOU CAN BUILD A SLIDING TRUMPET WITH TWO PIECES OF TUBING. ONE PIECE NEEDS TO FIT INTO THE OTHER. BLOW ON THE END OF THE SMALLER ONE AND SLIDE THE LARGER ONE.

TWO TUBES

A SLIDE TRUMPET

For some trumpeting musicians five notes were not enough to tell their stories. One solution for getting more tones with one instrument was to drill holes in the side of the trumpet tube. Instruments such as the wooden cornet and serpent used this system and were able to play many notes. The tone of some of the notes was not great, though, so the search went on.

Air Roadblocks, Sound Detour

The natural, slide, and keyed trumpets were made obsolete by the invention of the first valved trumpet. In 1818 Heinrich Stolzel and Friedrich Bluhmel of Berlin, Germany, were the first to patent a valve for the trumpet. Their patent was sold to some other instrument makers in Berlin who produced a two-valved trumpet. But their instrument was not very good, and the valved trumpet did not catch on right away. An Englishman, John Shaw, added springs to the valves in 1824. Another German, C. A. Muller, added a third valve a few years later. Francois Perinet finished the job in France in 1839 by producing an improved valve that is essentially the same as the one used in trumpets today. The addition of

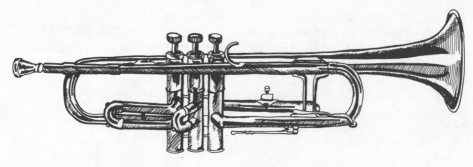

valves allowed trumpets to be shortened to about 4 feet of tube and still able to play a wide range of notes.

The valves on a trumpet work like roadblocks and detours on a street. When a street is blocked off and you detour around the block, the distance is longer than it would be if you could go straight down the street. The trumpet's valves divert the column of air through an extra length of tubing. This makes the vibrating column of air longer and the fundamental pitch lower.

The first valve on the trumpet lowers the pitch a full step. The second valve's tubing is half as long as the first and lowers the pitch a half step. The third valve increases the length of the column of air to about as long as the first and second valves combined, so it lowers the pitch a step and a half. When all three valves are opened, they lower the fundamental pitch three full steps.

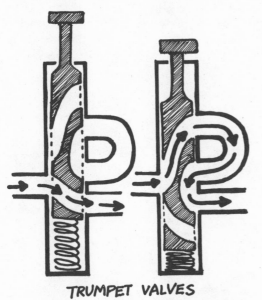

TRUMPET VALVES

Lip Reeding

Making reeds from cane requires some special equipment. Using drinking straws is less complicated, but

making a reed can be even simpler than that. In fact, you have an excellent double-beating reed with you right now. Look just below your nose—and just above your chin. There it is—your lips.

Somewhere, sometime, someone discovered that a nice buzzing sound could be made by wetting the lips, closing them in the position to say the letter "m," and blowing. Give it a try. If that method doesn't work, tense your cheek muscles, pull your closed lips back against your teeth, and blow again. Once you get a sound try relaxing your lips as you blow. How many different tones can you produce? Some professional musicians can actually play tunes on their lips alone. Pick a favorite old tune and try.

Blowing the lips is easy enough to do, and people must have enjoyed making noises this way. These days you may discover this activity is frowned upon in polite company, but it wasn't necessarily always that way.

When some people discover a noise, they seem compelled to make it louder. One such person long ago discovered that the lip buzz could be made louder by doing it into a hole in the side of a hollow animal horn. The musical horn was born.

By using different combinations of valves and changing the lip positions, the horn player can play many tones. The cup-shaped mouthpiece found on modern trumpets and horns helps the player to make clear tones. Mouthpieces come in different styles, which help players create special effects.

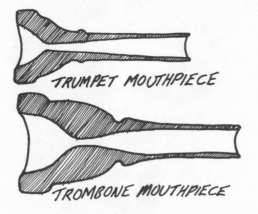

TRUMPET MOUTHPIECE

TROMBONE MOUTHPIECE

The tone of a trumpet or horn can also be changed by the use of a mute. Mutes are fitted into the bell (flared part) of the instrument to soften the tone or to produce unusual sounds.

A Bit About Horns

In all the family of instruments known as horns the diameter of the tubing gradually gets wider from the mouthpiece to the bell. But it hasn't always been like that. Before valves were added, either the music horn musicians could play was very limited or they had to use crooks (separate lengths of tubing) to increase the range of their instruments.

The crook horn had a selection of five detachable crooks. In order to keep the music flowing smoothly, the player had to develop the skill of changing crooks quickly.

Valves really saved the day. With valves, the player can change the length of the tubing by simply pressing a lever.

CROOK HORN AND THE FIVE CROOKS

One modern horn is called the French horn. It is actually a combination of two horns. One, the F horn, plays the low parts. For the high notes the player presses a thumb valve, so the horn will play in the key of B-flat. (As if this weren't enough, there is also a triple horn.)

French horn players hold their instruments by placing their right hand inside the bell. Changing the hand position helps to refine the sound of the instrument. The hand can also change the pitch of the horn or be used as a mute.

The tuba is a member of the horn family. It was first made in Berlin in the 1830s. Although the tuba has a very low voice, it can be used to play beautiful melodies.

The sousaphone, named after John Philip Sousa, is a large bass tuba especially adapted for marching bands. Sousa was famous as the composer of many popular marches, including "The Stars and Stripes Forever." The sousaphone is very visible because of its large bell. The player stands inside the coils of the instrument and supports it with his shoulder.

The trumpetlike cornet is a descendant of the post horn, a bugle played at horseraces. The cornet has a softer tone than the more brassy trumpet. The flugelhorn is a little larger than the cornet and has a mellow tone that is called for in jazz music.

Free Reeding

The harmonica, accordion, and their relatives make sound by the vibration of free reeds. The pitches of the

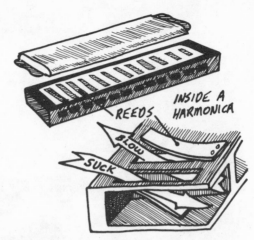

instrument are determined by the lengths of its reeds. For each tone there is a different reed.

The harmonica player's lips and tongue direct the stream of air to the proper reed. As the air passes by, the reed vibrates and creates a sound. In an accordion, keys and buttons help the player direct air from the bellows to the reed.

These two instruments are joined in this free-reeding family by the reed organ, melodica, pitchpipes, concertina, the Chinese sheng, the Japanese sho, and the Laotian khen.

Chapter 8
Body Music

Place your fingers at your throat and say a few words. You can feel your neck quiver. The quivers result as air, which you push up from your lungs, rushes against your vocal cords and causes them to vibrate. Try to hum or utter a sentence with your mouth shut tight and your nose pinched shut. Can you make beautiful sounds? Why won't your voice work?

Open your nose and try again to make a sound. Now close your nose and open your mouth as you try again to make the same noise. Do it several times in succession: nose, mouth, nose, mouth, nose, mouth. What are you saying? Do you think mothers taught their babies to say "mama" or that babies just beginning to make sounds taught their mothers? Check with someone you know who speaks another language and ask what babies call their mothers in that language. Can you guess what the word will be?

You have been playing with the most widely used musical instrument, the human voice. Human voices speak in many languages; people sing and hum millions of different tunes, but all voices work the same way.

Your voice organ (singers call it their instrument), is composed of your lungs, larynx, pharynx, mouth, and nose. The parts of your anatomy that make it possible for you to laugh, talk and sing are the same parts that make it possible for you to breathe, eat, and smell.

Your lungs produce a stream of air, which is forced up through your trachea, or windpipe, to your larynx, or voice box. At the bottom of your voice box are the two vocal folds. The vocal folds are often called "vocal cords," but they are actually folds about ½ inch long in the lining of your larynx. The opening between the two folds is called the glottis.

Put your fingers to your throat and feel the hard, slightly pointed bump. This is your Adam's apple, or thyroid cartilage. The front ends of your vocal folds attach to it.

The folds attach at the back to two small cartilages, which are able to move. The cartilages (called arytenoid cartilages) allow you to open the glottis for breathing and to close it and stretch the folds to make sounds. The closed folds also protect your lungs from small objects you might breathe in.

As air from your lungs is pushed between your closed, stretched vocal folds it causes them to vibrate. The train of rapid pulses of air that push through the vibrating folds and into the vocal tract is what you hear as voice.

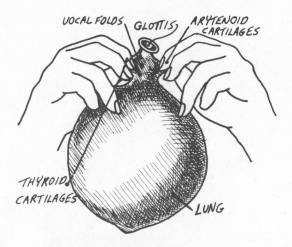

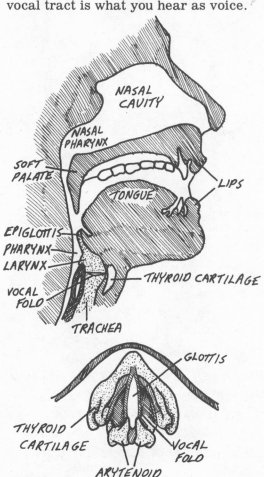

An Inhuman Voice

With a balloon you can make a model of the lungs and vocal folds. Blow up the balloon. Pinch the stem of it shut, using the thumb and first finger of both hands to grip it just below the opening. Imagine that the part of the balloon that is filled with air is a lung. Your left thumb and finger are the arytenoid cartilages; your right thumb and finger are your Adam's apple. The stem of the balloon stretched between your hands forms the folded lining of the larynx, your vocal folds.

As your cartilages (left thumb and finger) stretch the vocal folds (the stem of the balloon), force air from your lungs (the balloon) through them—a sound results. As the balloon sings, you can take a breath and sing along. As you allow the opening (glottis) in the stem of the balloon to widen, the balloon can exhale its air with a more relaxed "whoosh."

Some changes can be made in your voice by tightening and loosening the vocal folds or by pushing more or less air through them. You may have noticed this as you played with the squealing sound made by the pinched balloon. You may have also noticed that the voice of the balloon was not nearly as varied and gorgeous as yours was when you sang along. Credit the superior performance of your voice to the parts of your vocal organ, your fantastic brain, and your good taste in the way you use them.

The Vocal Tract

The cavern formed by your larynx, pharynx, mouth, and nose is the resonating chamber for the vibrations produced at the vocal folds. The shape and amount of air in this chamber and the sounds your voice will actually make can be changed by moving your lips, jaw, tongue, and larynx. Every change you make within the chamber results in a different sound.

Notice your tongue move as you talk or sing. Say "the." What did your tongue do? Did your jaw move? How about your lips?

Sing "la-la-la-la." Hum "Oh Susannah" or one of your favorite tunes

MAKE AN INHUMAN VOCAL TRACT

WITH A BALLOON AND A PIECE OF TUBING YOU CAN HEAR HOW DIFFERENT SIZE CHAMBERS CAN CHANGE THE TONE OF A SOUND. BEGIN BY CUTTING YOUR TUBE SO YOU HAVE DIFFERENT LE... PIECE A... LENGTH... OTHER IS A GOOD WAY.

SLIP THE MOUTH OF THE BALLOON OVER ONE END OF THE TUBE.

BLOW UP THE BALLOON AND HOLD THE AIR IN WITH A SOLID PINCH AS YOU TURN THE TUBE OVER.

HOLD THE TUBE BETWEEN YOUR KNEES WITH THE BALLOON END UP. NOW PINCH AND STRETCH THE BALLOON STEM TO FORM VOCAL FOLDS. ALLOW THE AIR FROM THE BALLOON TO PUSH THROUGH THE FOLDS AND LISTEN TO THE SOUND YOUR INSTRUMENT MAKES. HEAR THE DIFFERENCE IN TONE WHEN THE BALLOON SQUEALS WITHOUT A TUBE. USE ANOTHER LENGTH OF TUBE AND NOTICE THE DIFFERENT TONE.

and pay attention to the movements of your tongue, jaw, and lips. Say these tongue twisters and notice how your mouth parts move to make the words.

If Peter Piper picked a peck of pickled peppers, how many pecks of pickled peppers would Peter Piper pick?
She sells seashells by the sea-shore.

As you are speaking or singing, your vocal cords are producing a squeal much like a pinched balloon. With your vocal tract you select and form the sounds that finally emerge from your nose and mouth.

The inhuman vocal tract illustrates how your vocal tract works, but it is not a very practical instrument. Imagine some ways you could make it into a musical instrument capable of playing a variety of notes in rapid succession.

Warning: You may notice that as you experiment with the inhuman vocal tract that parents, teachers, pets, and even true friends may treat you as if *you* were not quite human. Remember that one person's music can be another's idea of noise. Be considerate.

Making a Musical You

Your body is loaded with musical potential. Some of its sounds—the beat of your heart, blood squirting through your veins, breathing, grunts, groans, and stomach gurgling—happen without your having a lot of control. Other sounds you make and hear only when you are sick. You may have noticed that other people make some interesting sounds when they are asleep. (You probably do too.) The voice is the most obvious source of sound from the human body. But there are other ways the musical you can be played.

You are an idiophone, aerophone, and membranophone. You don't have to build or even pick up anything to be a musical you. Slap, tap, whistle, scrape, clap, tromp, and thud are just some of the sounds you can make with your body.

Think about the parts of your body and what sounds they might make. One way is to start at your toes and check out each part as you go up to the top of your head. With your imagination cruise back down your body to see if you missed some sounds on the way up. Try yourself out: you probably sound pretty good.

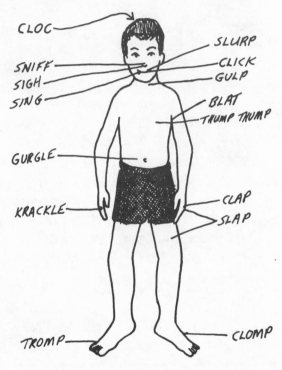

Your brain makes the musical you musical. That is the place where the difference between music and noise is decided. The decision is up to you. There are ideas and opinions (some are taken very seriously) in any culture about what is music and what isn't. Those ideas continually change. When a person is able to tell his or her story clearly, using what everybody had always thought was only noise, that noise becomes music.

117

THE SUPER-COLOSSAL MUSICAL-YOU BAND

YOU, WITH A LITTLE HELP FROM YOUR FRIENDS, CAN MAKE A MUSICAL-YOU BAND. GATHER TOGETHER A BUNCH OF MUSICAL YOUS. EACH OF YOUR FRIENDS IS ONE. WHEN YOU HAVE TWO OR MORE WILLING MUSICAL-YOUS, A BAND IS POSSIBLE. CHOOSE A LEADER, OR STARTER. THIS PERSON WILL START BY PLAYING A REGULAR BEAT OR RHYTHM ON HIS OR HER MUSICAL YOU-KNOW-WHAT. ONE BY ONE THE OTHER MUSICIANS JOIN IN. AS EACH NEW MUSICIAN JOINS THE BAND, HE OR SHE SHOULD ADD JUST THE RHYTHM OR SOUND HE THINKS THE BAND NEEDS. BY THE TIME SEVERAL CAREFUL CHOICES HAVE BEEN MADE THE BAND SHOULD BE SOUNDING GREAT.

ONCE THE MUSIC IS GOING, THE LEADER CAN POINT OUT PARTICULAR "YOUSICIANS" TO IMPROVISE (MAKE UP AS YOU PLAY) A SOLO (ALONE). THE OTHERS PLAY QUIETLY WHILE THE SOLOIST PLAYS LOUDER. GO AROUND THE BAND AND GIVE EACH "YOUSICIAN" A CHANCE TO SOLO.

A COMPOSITION FOR A MUSICAL-YOU BAND

ONE WAY TO MAKE MUSIC IS TO JUST START AND SEE WHAT HAPPENS. ANOTHER WAY IS TO HAVE AN IDEA OR A PARTICULAR STORY YOU WANT TO SHARE, THEN CHOOSE AND ARRANGE THE SOUNDS THAT WILL BEST EXPRESS YOUR IDEA. WHEN YOU CHOOSE AND ARRANGE SOUNDS TO GET THE RESULTS YOU WANT, YOU ARE MAKING A COMPOSITION, OR COMPOSING. MANY SONGS ARE WRITTEN THIS WAY. (CONTINUED)

A COMPOSITION FOR
A MUSICAL-YOU BAND
(CONTINUED)

YOU CAN COMPOSE PIECES FOR YOUR MUSICAL-YOU BAND TO PLAY. HERE IS A COMPOSITION YOU CAN TRY TO SEE HOW IT IS DONE.

THIS PIECE WORKS BEST IF THE YOU-BAND HAS EIGHT OR MORE MUSICIANS AND A LEADER, OR CONDUCTOR. THE CONDUCTOR DIVIDES THE "YOUSICIANS" INTO TWO GROUPS, GROUP 1 AND GROUP 2. TO TELL THEM WHAT AND WHEN TO PLAY THE CONDUCTOR USES HAND SIGNALS.

THE HAND HELD FLAT WITH THE EDGE SHOWING MEANS RUB YOUR PALMS TOGETHER.

THE FLAT PALM SHOWING MEANS SLAP YOUR HANDS ON YOUR THIGHS.

A CLENCHED FIST MEANS STOMP YOUR FEET AND POUND THE TABLE.

THE CONDUCTOR CHECKS TO SEE THAT EVERYBODY UNDERSTANDS THE SIGNALS. GROUP 1 WILL WATCH THE LEFT HAND, GROUP 2 THE RIGHT. THE CONDUCTOR COUNTS 1-2-3-4-5, 1-2-3-4-5, SILENTLY AND CHANGES THE SIGNALS EVERY FIVE SECONDS.

	GROUP	SIGNAL	ACTION
(A) 5 SEC	GROUP 1	▮	BEGINS RUBBING
	GROUP 2		SILENT
(B) 5 SEC	GROUP 1	▮	CONTINUES RUBBING
	GROUP 2	▮	STARTS RUBBING
(C) 5 SEC	GROUP 1	▮	STARTS SLAPPING
	GROUP 2	▮	CONTINUES RUBBING
(D) 5 SEC	GROUP 1	▮	CONTINUES SLAPPING
	GROUP 2	▮	STARTS SLAPPING
(E) 5 SEC	GROUP 1	▬	STOMPS AND POUNDS
	GROUP 2	▮	CONTINUES SLAPPING
(F) 5 SEC	GROUP 1	▬	CONTINUES STOMPS
	GROUP 2	▬	STARTS STOMPS
(G) 5 SEC	GROUP 1	▮	SLAPS AGAIN
	GROUP 2	▮	CONTINUES STOMPS
(H) 5 SEC	GROUP 1	▮	CONTINUES SLAPPING
	GROUP 2	▮	STARTS SLAPPING
(I) 5 SEC	GROUP 1	▮	STARTS RUBBING
	GROUP 2	▮	CONTINUES SLAPPING
(J) 5 SEC	GROUP 1	▮	CONTINUES RUBBING
	GROUP 2	▮	STARTS RUBBING
(K) 5 SEC	GROUP 1		SILENT
	GROUP 2	▮	CONTINUES RUBBING
ALL	SILENCE		

THIS COMPOSITION SOUNDS LIKE A SUMMER RAIN. FIRST THERE IS A DRIZZLE, THEN A LIGHT RAIN PITTER-PATTERING. NEXT IT STARTS TO RAIN VERY HARD. THEN THE STORM SOFTENS INTO THE SILENCE AFTER THE STORM BEFORE THE SUN BURSTS OUT.

THINK OF SOME SOUND STORIES YOU COULD TELL TO OR WITH YOUR MUSICAL FRIENDS. YOU CAN MAKE UP YOU-BAND GUESSING GAMES. MAKE COMPOSITIONS THAT CLEARLY EXPRESS YOUR IDEAS TO OTHERS.

P.S. HAVE FUN.

Chapter 9

Musical Notations

We use language to write stories or books. The words in this book tell you my thoughts as I write. You may be reading them years after I write them, but my thoughts at this moment are recorded here where I can share them with you. Written language makes it possible. You and I have both learned a code. We began by learning an alphabet, then how to make words and sentences. Somewhere in the process we learned to use the code to express our thoughts, wants, and ideas to others. A written code allows us to share ideas with people we may never see. It even allows us to communicate with other people after we are dead.

A written idea can be carried all over the world and can last for centuries. Music, too, can be written as a code to be deciphered, studied, and played at a later date. A code or language about music must be learned by both the writer and the reader. Just as there are many languages and verbal codes, there are also many codes of musical notation. You and your friends could make up a system of music notation all your own.

A system of music notation must tell the musician what pitch to play, what instrument to play it on, how loud the sound should be, how long it should last, and what character (timbre) it should have. If a musician or a composer tried to explain all that information with words, it would take pages just to tell how to play a few notes. Long compositions, such as a symphony, in which many musicians are playing at the same time, would take volumes to explain with words. Musicians would have to read super fast.

In the system of notation used in the Western world a special picture is drawn and written so the musicians can quickly understand what the composer had in mind and play it.

Good musicians can read sheet music and hear the sounds in their heads. They can do this as easily as you can read words on a page and imagine people talking or see pictures in your mind.

Conductors of orchestras must know what many different instruments are doing all at the same time. They read the information from a "score." On the pages of the score the staffs for each instrument are arranged one under the next down the page. After studying the score, the conductor knows at a glance or memorizes what sounds should be going on when. The conductor helps the musicians play together by beating time with his or her arms.

MUSICAL NOTATION

THE "STAFF" HAS FIVE PARALLEL, HORIZONTAL LINES. THE LINES AND THE SPACES BETWEEN THEM REPRESENT DIFFERENT PITCHES. SPECIAL MARKS CALLED "NOTES" ARE DRAWN ON THE STAFF. EACH NOTE HAS A TIME VALUE. ITS SHAPE TELLS THE MUSICIAN HOW LONG TO PLAY A PITCH. THEIR LOCATION ON THE STAFF TELLS THE MUSICIAN WHAT PITCH TO PLAY

STAFF WITH SOME NOTES

THE LINES AND SPACES HAVE LETTER NAMES, A, B, C, D, E, F, AND G. THESE SAME SEVEN LETTERS REPEAT UP THE STAFF. AS A LETTER REPEATS UP THE STAFF THE PITCH PLAYED DOUBLES. IF ONE "A" VIBRATES 440 TIMES A SECOND, THE "A" ABOVE IT ON THE STAFF VIBRATES 880 TIMES A SECOND.

NOT ALL STAFFS REPRESENT THE SAME GROUP OF PITCHES. AT THE LEFT END OF THE STAFF IS A MARK CALLED A "CLEF." THE TWO MOST COMMON ARE THE BASS CLEF AND THE TREBLE CLEF. THE CLEF TELLS WHICH RANGE OF PITCHES THE COMPOSER WANTS THE MUSICIAN TO USE.

TREBLE CLEF   BASS CLEF

SPACED ALONG THE STAFF ARE VERTICAL LINES GOING FROM TOP TO BOTTOM. THESE LINES ARE CALLED BARS. THEY REPRESENT INTERVALS OF TIME JUST LIKE THE MARKS ON A CLOCK. MUSICIANS COUNT AS THEY PLAY THEIR INSTRUMENTS. THEY ARRIVE AT A BAR EVERY TIME THEY COUNT A CERTAIN NUMBER OF BEATS. AT THE LEFT END OF THE FIRST STAFF IN A PIECE OF MUSIC THERE ARE TWO NUMBERS, ONE ON TOP OF THE OTHER. THE TOP NUMBER TELLS HOW MANY BEATS THERE ARE BETWEEN BARS. THE BOTTOM ONE TELLS WHAT KIND OF NOTE GETS (EQUALS) ONE BEAT.

BARS

TIME SIGNATURE   p   ff

ABOVE AND BELOW THE STAFF VARIOUS WORDS AND SYMBOLS ARE WRITTEN AND DRAWN IN. THEY GIVE INSTRUCTIONS ABOUT HOW LOUD OR SOFTLY TO PLAY. THEY ALSO GIVE INFORMATION ABOUT THE CHARACTER OF THE SOUNDS.

PUT IT ALL TOGETHER AND "MARY HAD A LITTLE LAMB" LOOKS LIKE THIS:

SYMBOL GUESSING

MAKE A LIST OF SOUND WORDS. DRAW A SYMBOL THAT YOU THINK LOOKS LIKE
EACH WORD SOUNDS. SHOW A FRIEND OR FRIENDS THE SYMBOLS AND SEE IF
THEY CAN GUESS THE SOUNDS YOU HAD IN MIND. TRY MAKING THE SYMBOLS
REALLY LOOK LIKE THE SOUNDS. NO FAIR USING ONOMATOPOEIA!

HOW TO MAKE A COMPOSITION BOARD

THIS IS A SYSTEM OF MUSICAL NOTATION
YOU CAN MAKE AND PLAY WITH YOUR
FRIENDS OR YOUR MUSICAL-YOU
BAND. EACH PERSON THINKS OF A
SOUND, OR YOU CAN USE NAMES.
MAKE A SYMBOL FOR EACH SOUND
OR NAME. TRY TO MAKE ONE
THAT LOOKS LIKE THE SOUND. PUT
THE SYMBOLS ON SMALL PIECES
OF PAPER THAT WILL FIT INTO
BOXES OF A GRID.

MAKE A GRID THAT EVERY-
ONE CAN SEE ON A LARGE
PIECE OF PAPER.

IN THE BOXES OF THE GRID PUT
THE SYMBOLS OF THE SOUNDS.
PUT JUST ONE SYMBOL IN EACH

BOX FOR STARTERS. LEAVE SOME
BOXES EMPTY TO REPRESENT
SILENCE IF YOU WANT.

CHOOSE ONE PERSON TO BE THE
CONDUCTOR. THE CONDUCTOR COUNTS
EVENLY AND POINTS FROM ONE
BOX TO THE NEXT FOR EACH BEAT.
WHEN THE CONDUCTOR POINTS TO
A BOX WITH A SYMBOL, THE PERSON
WHOSE SOUND IT REPRESENTS
MAKES THE SOUND. GO THROUGH
THE COMPOSITION SEVERAL TIMES
UNTIL YOU CAN DO IT EASILY.

CHANGE THE SYMBOLS AROUND
AND PUT TWO OR THREE IN SOME
BOXES AND SEE HOW IT GOES.
ADD NEW SOUNDS SO EACH PERSON
HAS TWO OR MORE TO MAKE. HAVE
THE CONDUCTOR INDICATE LOUD
AND SOFT BY RAISING AND LOWERING
HIS OR HER HAND. TRY GOING FAST
AND SLOW. MAKE IMPROVEMENTS
YOU THINK MIGHT HELP THE SYSTEM
WORK OR SOUND BETTER.

USE YOUR INSTRUMENTS.

Chapter 10

Science, Music, and You

When you turn on your radio or record player, the sounds that come to your ears have been reproduced electronically by the machine. In each case the sound has been changed by a machine into electronic impulses. Electronic impulses can travel more easily than sound. They can also be stored on disks (records) or tapes to be reproduced into sound at a later date. The patterns of the impulses can be decoded by other machines to make sound again.

There is a whole new world of sounds being explored by musicians and scientists. Sounds are created electronically. Instead of blowing, strumming, hitting, or bowing, the musician turns knobs and flips switches. Electronic equipment allows composers to create sounds and compositions of sounds directly. The composition is directly encoded on a magnetic tape and is immediately ready for replay. With one or several machines the composer can write and play a symphony all by him- or herself.

Impulses of electricity are generated, distorted, filtered, and amplified to make new and interesting sounds. Musicians have a vast new source of sounds and equipment to help them tell their stories.

Through science we have come to

understand more and more the building blocks of life and have discovered a kind of music in all life. The cells, molecules, atoms of your body vibrate at different pitches and in groups to make up you. Without bowing, blowing, or hitting anything you are already and constantly music. Because you are music, the music made by musicians affects you. It mixes with your cells and blood and becomes part of what you are.

Scientists have found that certain music, such as the music of Bach, helps plants grow faster and stay healthy. Music helps sick people become well. Some sounds disrupt and disturb the health of people and plants. Much remains to be discovered about the music we make and the music that is everywhere waiting for us to notice. We are an important part of the music of the world.

You've come to the end of this book. But your voyage of musical discovery is really just beginning. Hear and play the world. You musical you!

Some Books About Musical Instruments

Here are a few of the many books about musical instruments that I have come across in my explorations. Some were used in the preparation of this book. Some I discovered after the book was written. You may find others as well that are useful to your explorations. Check libraries for other books that will stir your musical imagination.

Banek, Reinhold, and Scoville, Jon. *Sound Designs*. Berkeley: Ten Speed Press, 1980. An adult book showing how to make instruments, mostly percussion types. Has a spirit of invention and encourages the use of recycled materials.

Berger, Melvin. *The Trumpet Book*. New York: Lothrop, Lee & Shepard, 1978. A book for young people about trumpets. Includes photos showing how trumpets are made. Contains all kinds of other trumpet information.

Cline, Dallas. *Cornstalk Fiddle and Other Homemade Instruments*. New York: Oak Publications, 1976. Step-by-step illustrations on how to make more than 30 musical instruments from easy-to-find materials.

_____. *How to Play Nearly Everything*. New York: Oak Publications, 1977. Good instructions with photographs and some illustrations on how to play ten folk instruments.

Diagram Group. *Musical Instruments of the World*. New York: Paddington Press, 1976. This amazing book has more than 4000 drawings of musical instruments and was the source of several of the drawings adapted for this book. For a look at the vast array of possibilities in musical instruments this book is a must. It gives an inspiring insight into the imaginations of people around the world.

Hunter, Ilene, and Judson, Marilyn. *Simple Folk Instruments to Make and Play*. New York: Simon & Schuster, 1977. A recipe book telling how to make about a hundred simple musical instruments.

Jeans, Sir James. *Science and Music*. New York: Dover Publications, 1936, 1968. An adult book about the science of musical sounds. Good, understandable information for adult readers.

Kettlekamp, Larry. *Horns. Drums, Rattles, and Bells. Flutes, Whistles, and Reeds. Singing Strings*. New York: William Morrow & Co. These children's books give excellent information about instruments, how they work, and their history. Good for basic information.

Mason, Bernard S. *Drums, Tomtoms, and Rattles*. New York: Dover Publications, 1938, 1974. A good look into American Indian lore and the making of drums and rattles.

Partch, Harry. *Genesis of a Music*. New York: Da Capo Press, 1949, 1974. Harry Partch was a composer who wrote a music of his own, based on harmonics, and invented instruments on which to play it. In this adult book he tells the stories and dimensions of his amazing instruments. The pictures alone are an adventure.

Reck, David. *Music of the Whole Earth*. New York: Charles Scribner's Sons, 1977. A large musicology book for adults. It has lots of photos of musicians and instruments from around the world. The text and diagrams are somewhat technical, but if you are interested in the music of the world, this is a very good book.

Sawyer, David. *Vibrations*. New York: Cambridge University Press, 1977. An adult how-to-book showing how to make unconventional musical instruments. Good illustrations, photos, and instructions and good for your imagination.

Schafer, R. Murray. *The Composer in the Classroom. Ear Cleaning. The New Soundscape. When Words Sing*. New York: Associated Music Publishers, 1965-1970. Mr. Schafer is a Canadian composer and teacher. His booklets are condensed from his college-level classes. They take a fresh, imaginative look into the world of musical possibilities.

Scott, John M. *What Is Sound?* New York: Parents' Magazine Press, 1973. A young reader's introduction to the science of sound.

Scientific American. *The Physics of Music*. San Francisco: W. H. Freeman & Co., 1978. A book of articles about the physics of music reprinted from *Scientific American* magazine. Very interesting, illustrated adult technical reading.

Seeger, Peter. *Henscratches and Flyspecks*. New York: Berkeley Medallion Books, 1973. Tells how to read melodies from songbooks. Adult reading level.

Seeger, Peter. *The Incomplete Folksinger*. New York: Simon & Schuster, 1972. The folksinger tells about his life and the music, musicians, and instruments he knows. Adult reading level.